Home/Community Connections

TABLE OF CONTENTS

OVERVIEW _____ 2

Section 1 — **Communicating with Parents**
Introduction _____ 5
▲ Welcome Letters _____ 9
❖ Student Inventory (Form) _____ 15
❖ Theme Newsletters _____ 17
❖ Parent-Teacher Conferences Request for Information (Form) ___ 29
Parent-Teacher Conference Outline (Form) _____ 31
Post-Conference Action Plan (Form) _____ 32

Section 2 — **Parents and Teachers Working as Partners**
Introduction _____ 33
❖ Family Homework _____ 35
❖ Home Projects _____ 47
❖ Home Project Evaluation (Form) _____ 71
❖ Parent-Teacher-Child Dialogue (Form) _____ 73
❖ Parent Articles _____ 75
❖ School's Out! (End-of-Year Books/Activities) _____ 85

Section 3 — **Using Volunteers in the Classroom**
Introduction _____ 87
Request for Volunteers (Form) _____ 90
Volunteer Topics (Form) _____ 91
Volunteer Handbook _____ 93
Volunteer Certificate (Form) _____ 102

Section 4 — **Moving Beyond the Classroom**
Introduction _____ 103
A Family Reading Program _____ 104
❖ Reading Contract (Form) _____ 107
Parent Book List _____ 109
Sharing Family Stories _____ 111
Conducting a Workshop _____ 113
Setting Up a Parent Resource Center _____ 115
Working with the Community _____ 117
Starting a Homework Club _____ 119

Assessing Your Home/Community Program _____ 120

❖ = Appears in English and Spanish

▲ = Appears in English, Spanish, Cambodian, Chinese, Hmong, and Vietnamese

Home/Community Connections

OVERVIEW

HOME/COMMUNITY CONNECTIONS provides all the resources you need to construct the home-school partnership that will result in improved school learning for your students.

Section 1

Communicating with Parents

Resources for establishing and maintaining contact with parents

- Welcome Letters
- Student Inventory
- Theme Newsletters
- Parent-Teacher Conferences Request for Information
- Parent-Teacher Conference Outline
- Post-Conference Action Plan

Section 2

Parents and Teachers Working as Partners

A variety of ideas for actively involving parents in their children's reading education

- Family Homework
- Home Projects and Evaluation Form
- Parent-Teacher-Child Dialogue Form
- Parent Articles
- School's Out!

Section 3

Using Volunteers in the Classroom

Ideas and resources for identifying, training, and managing volunteers in the classroom

- Request for Volunteers
- Volunteer Topics
- Volunteer Handbook
- Volunteer Certificate

Section 4

Moving Beyond the Classroom

Information for starting or expanding a number of programs

- A Family Reading Program
- Reading Contract
- Parent Book List
- Sharing Family Stories
- Conducting a Workshop
- Setting Up a Parent Resource Center
- Working with the Community
- Starting a Homework Club

As you become familiar with HOME/COMMUNITY CONNECTIONS, you will be able to determine quickly which resources you want to use and when to send material home. The information below will help you get started.

Welcome Letter and Student Inventory

- During Open House
- At Back-to-School Night
- Or, during the first week of school

Theme Newsletter

- When students begin reading the theme

Home Project and Evaluation Form

- When students begin reading the second selection of the theme
  This will give parents and students 2 to 3 weeks to complete the project.

Family Homework

- When students begin reading the third and fourth selections in the theme
  This will give parents and students 1 to 2 weeks to prepare for the upcoming theme.

Communicating with Parents

Section One of *Home/Community Connections* includes ideas to help you communicate with parents. Included are letters that invite parents to be active participants in their child's education, forms that ask them to provide information to help you work with their child, and newsletters that update them on the themes you're reading in class. Included also are forms and information that you can use to facilitate communication at parent-teacher conferences.

Similar forms and information are provided on the Teacher's Resource Disks, which you can personalize by making deletions, adding personal messages, and adjusting the contents. Items on the Teacher's Resource Disks are indicated with an icon. Additional resources for communicating with parents can be found in the *Teacher's Book,* the *Teacher's Assessment Handbook,* the *Language Resources Teacher's Booklet,* and the *Extra Support Handbook.*

❖ = Appears in English and Spanish

▣ = Teacher's Resource Disks

TABLE OF CONTENTS FOR SECTION 1

Introduction ——————————————— 6
    Establishing and Maintaining Contact with Parents
    Gathering Student Information and Putting It to Use
    Planning and Conducting Parent-Teacher Conferences
    Related Reading

Welcome Letter to Parents
    English ——————————————— 9
    Spanish ——————————————— 10
    Vietnamese ——————————————— 11
    Hmong ——————————————— 12
    Chinese ——————————————— 13
    Cambodian ——————————————— 14

Student Inventory ——————————————— 15

❖ **Theme Newsletters**
    Oink, Oink, Oink ——————————————— 17
    Community Ties ——————————————— 19
    Disaster! ——————————————— 21
    What's Cooking? ——————————————— 23
    Weather Watch ——————————————— 25
    What a Day! ——————————————— 27

❖ **Parent-Teacher Conference Request for Information** ——————— 29

Parent-Teacher Conference Outline ——————————————— 31

Post-Conference Action Plan ——————————————— 32

Establishing and Maintaining Contact with Parents

Communication between parents and teachers is very important to a child's success in school. Certain changes in family life in recent years can make contact with parents more difficult. Families who have immigrated recently may not yet speak or read English. Many parents' jobs make lack of time another serious obstacle to overcome. Still, family involvement is as important as ever. This section includes a variety of resources to help you reach parents. You can use these resources in whatever way is appropriate for your particular group of students and parents.

Welcome Letter to Parents The Welcome Letter, in English, Spanish, Vietnamese, Hmong, Chinese, and Cambodian on pages 9–14, can be used to establish your initial contact with parents. This letter invites parents to participate in their child's education, lets them know about the activities they will be asked to do with their child, tells parents how they can help their child with reading, and makes a special request for bilingual volunteers. (The Request for Volunteers, on page 90 of Section 3, can also be used to identify people willing and able to provide you with bilingual assistance.)

The Welcome Letter translations provide an opportunity to establish communication with parents who speak a language other than English. These letters differ from the English letter in that they also ask parents whether they need all materials sent home throughout the year to be translated, providing a section at the bottom that parents can fill out to request this. The letter also reassures them that reading in their home language is as helpful to their child as reading in English.

Theme Newsletters The six theme newsletters, one for each of the themes children will be reading, can be used to maintain contact with parents throughout the year. The newsletters give an overview of the theme, provide lists of theme-related books, and suggest theme-related activities for parents and children to do together. The newsletters appear in English and Spanish on pages 17–28.

Gathering Student Information and Putting It to Use

Student Inventory The Student Inventory, in English and Spanish on pages 15 and 16, asks parents to provide information about their child's school history, language background, reading habits, and interests. This information will give you a better understanding of your students and can be put to practical use when assessing needs, suggesting outside reading, and organizing groups according to interests. The Student Inventory could be sent home with the Welcome Letter to Parents, or you may wish to give it out at an Open House or Back-to-School Night.

Planning and Conducting Parent-Teacher Conferences

Planning Conferences Regular parent conferences are an important part of the communication between home and school. Consider these suggestions as you plan conferences:

• Schedule conferences at times that are convenient for parents. Many children live with working parents who may find it difficult to meet during regular school hours. By being flexible when arranging a time to meet, you can encourage these parents to participate.

• The need to care for younger siblings may be keeping parents at home. If it is possible to arrange for child supervision and entertainment during the conference, invite the younger siblings to come along.

• Depending on the cultural diversity of your

school, you may have a few or many parents who are not fluent in English. This lack of English proficiency prevents them from understanding what is being discussed and from explaining their views. Help parents who speak a language other than English by inviting them to bring someone who can serve as an interpreter during the conference. If you can assist in such arrangements, offer to help. Or, encourage your school to subscribe to AT&T Language Line Services, which provides access to interpreters from English into approximately 140 languages. This service allows you to talk to a non-English-speaking parent through an interpreter over the phone, or to meet face to face with a parent while your "invisible" translator joins you on a speaker phone. For more information, call AT&T Language Line Services at 1 800 752-6096.

Parent-Teacher Conference Request for Information

If you can provide flexibility in scheduling your conferences, the form on pages 29–30 can be sent to parents before conferences are scheduled to gather information about parents' special needs. It provides an opportunity to find out the best time to schedule the conference, and whether a translator, child care, or transportation will make the difference in whether a parent can attend the conference. If any options are included on it that you cannot provide, simply mask them out before making copies to send home.

Making Parents Feel Comfortable
There are a number of things you can do to put parents at ease. Consider these suggestions:

- Make the conference area as comfortable as possible by providing adult-sized chairs instead of child-sized chairs.

- Greet parents at the door and sit with them at a table or in facing chairs instead of sitting behind your desk.

- Show that you think the conference is important and value their time by hanging a "Conference in Session" sign on the door to avoid interruptions.

- Be sensitive to cultural differences and how they affect communications. For example, "yes" doesn't always mean an affirmative reply in some cultures, but merely that a

message has been heard. If you are unsure of the meaning of a "yes" response, ask parents specifically what they think in order to get a clearer picture of their views, or involve a translator to avoid misunderstandings. Be alert, too, for cultural and social differences related to eye contact, personal space, silence, and space between speaker and listener that may give rise to uncomfortable moments.

Parent-Teacher Conference Outline
The Parent-Teacher Conference Outline on page 31 offers you a planning tool as well as a suggested structure for the conference. It will move you through the following important points of a conference:

- sharing the child's selected portfolio materials
- asking for parents' assessment of their child
- sharing your own assessment of the child
- discussing the child's areas of strength and areas in need of support
- formulating a plan for how you and the parents can work together to help the child both in school and at home

Including Students in the Conference
You may want to consider involving the child in the conference. You can decide the degree to which the child is to be involved, or you may want to let him or her decide. Some children may prefer to listen only. Others may be interested in more active involvement by reflecting on their own learning, preparing and presenting their portfolios, responding to teacher or parent assessments, and offering their own assessment of themselves.

Post-Conference Action Plan
Use the Post-Conference Action Plan on page 32 to jot down notes during the conference, record your notes after the conference, and summarize any information you learned about the child from the parents that will help you reach the child. It will help you keep track of parents' concerns and the plans and commitments you come up with together to help the child. The Action Plan will also provide useful information when it is time to prepare for the next conference.

Related Reading

Changing the View: Student-Led Parent Conferences,
Terri Austin. Heinemann, 1994. An experienced
teacher in Fairbanks, Alaska, shares her success
with having students take responsibility for lead-
ing their own parent conferences.

"Giving Students a Voice at Conference Time,"
Suzanne Moyers. *Instructor*, October 1994, p. 64.
Teachers at a school in Piedmont, California,
encourage students to present their portfolios to
their parents at conference time.

"Student/Parent Conferences: A New Generation,"
Stacy Kasse. *Teaching K-8*, November/December
1994, p. 78. A teacher in Medford, New Jersey,

experiments with student/parent conferences
and discovers the benefits for students, parents,
and teachers.

"Why Some Parents Don't Come to School," Margaret
Finders and Cynthia Lewis. *Educational
Leadership*, May 1994, p. 50.

The Houghton Mifflin education center located
on the Internet is a free online service that lists
useful articles from the ERIC Digest. Access the
education center through the School Division
Home Page on Houghton Mifflin's World Wide
Web site. The URL address:
http://www.hmco.com/school/

Dear Family,

Welcome . . . to the new school year. I would like to invite you to help me make this an exciting and successful year for your child. Studies have shown that children who get support in reading and learning at home do better in school. In order for schools to be successful, families and teachers must work together.

One of the things I will be asking you to do is to give me information that will help me get to know your child better. And throughout the year, I will be sending home ideas for activities that you and your child can do together. The activities will help your child with what we are studying in school. Please become involved as much as you can.

Of all the things you can do to help your child at home, the two most important are:

- **Read and discuss books together.** You can read to your child, your child can read to you, or you can read together. Visit the library together so you can select books that both of you will enjoy.

- **Let your child see you reading.** This will show your child that you think reading is valuable and enjoyable.

I also have a special request. If you are bilingual in English and another language, please let me know if you would be willing to assist families who speak your other language.

Thank you for working with me as a partner in your child's education.

Sincerely,

_____

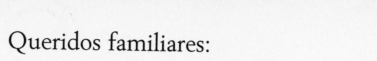

Queridos familiares:

¡Bienvenidos... al nuevo año escolar! Quisiera comenzar pidiéndoles su colaboración para que su niño/a tenga una experiencia emocionante y exitosa este año. Se ha comprobado que los estudiantes que alcanzan un mejor rendimiento escolar son los que más ayuda reciben en sus hogares para aprender a leer y otras destrezas. El éxito en la escuela se logra cuando los familiares y los maestros trabajamos juntos.

Para poder conocer mejor a su niño/a, les voy a pedir que me cuenten algo sobre él/ella. A lo largo del año, les iré enviando ideas de actividades para la casa (en español) que ustedes y su niño/a pueden hacer juntos. Estas actividades reforzarán los temas que estudiamos en la escuela. Por favor, participen lo más que puedan. (Tal vez envíe algunos materiales en inglés. Pero si necesitan todos los materiales traducidos al español, por favor completen la última parte de esta hoja y envíenla a la escuenla. Trataré de que un maestro o asistente bilingüe se ponga en contacto con ustedes.)

Entre la gran variedad de cosas que pueden hacer en casa para ayudar a su niño/a, las dos más importantes son:

- **Leer libros y conversar sobre lo que leen.** Los adultos pueden leerles a los niños, los niños a los adultos o turnarse para leer. Ustedes y su niño/a pueden ir juntos a la biblioteca y escoger libros, escritos en inglés o español, que les gusten a ambos.

- **Hacer que su niño/a vea que ustedes leen.** Esto le demostrará que ustedes valoran la lectura y disfrutan de ella. El idioma en el que ustedes lean no importa; lo que cuenta es el hecho de leer.

Voy a pedirles también algo muy especial: si hablan inglés y español, por favor avísenme si están dispuestos/as a ayudar a familia que hablan español únicamente.

Gracias por colaborar conmigo en la tarea de educar a su niño/a.

Atentamente,

_____

Por favor, trate de que alguien traduzca los materiales al español.

Nombre _____ Teléfono _____

Gia đình thân mến,

Chào mừng ... đến niên học mới. Tôi muốn mời ông bà giúp tôi làm năm học này được vui vẻ và thành công cho con ông bà. Sự nghiên cứu đã cho thấy rằng các em nào có sự ủng hộ trong khi đọc và học ở nhà thì học giỏi ở trường. Để cho các trường được thành công, các gia đình và thầy giáo phải làm việc với nhau.

Một trong những điều tôi sẽ hỏi ông bà làm là cho tôi chi tiết mà sẽ giúp tôi làm quen với con ông bà rõ hơn. Và trong năm, tôi sẽ gởi về nhà các ý kiến cho sinh hoạt mà ông bà và cháu có thể làm cùng nhau. Các sinh hoạt sẽ giúp cháu về những gì chúng ta đang học ở trường. Xin ông bà tham dự càng nhiều càng tốt. (Tài liệu tôi gởi về nhà sẽ là bằng tiếng Anh. Nếu ông bà cần thông dịch qua tiếng mẹ đẻ, xin điền đơn dưới đây và gởi lại trường. Tôi sẽ cố thu xếp cho một thầy giáo song ngữ hoặc người phụ tá để giúp ông bà.)

Trong tất cả những gì mà ông bà có thể làm để giúp cháu ở nhà, hai điều quan trọng nhất là:

• **Đọc và đàm thoại sách cùng nhau.** Ông bà có thể đọc cho cháu, cháu có thể đọc cho ông bà, hay cả hai đọc cùng nhau. Đi ra thư viện cùng nhau để ông bà và cháu có thể chọn sách mà cả hai đều thích. Các sách mà ông bà và cháu đọc có thể được viết bằng tiếng Anh hay bằng tiếng mẹ đẻ.

• **Cho cháu thấy ông bà đọc.** Điều này sẽ cho cháu thấy là ông bà nghĩ đọc là quí báu và thích thú. Thêm nữa, mặc dù ông bà đọc tiếng mẹ đẻ hay tiếng Anh không là quan trọng. Chỉ nhìn thấy ông bà đọc là rất quan trọng cho cháu.

Tôi cũng có một sự yêu cầu đặc biệt. Nếu ông bà thạo cả tiếng mẹ đẻ và Anh ngữ, xin cho tôi biết nếu ông bà sẵn sàng giúp các gia đình khác mà nói tiếng của ông bà.

Cám ơn sự cộng tác của ông bà với tôi trong sự giáo dục của cháu.

Trân thành,

_____

Nếu được, xin thu xếp cho người nào thông dịch tài liệu cho tôi.

Tiếng mẹ đẻ của tôi là _____

Tên_____ Điện thoại _____

Nyob zoo tsev tuab neeg,

Zoo sab txais tog mej rua kev kawm ntawv rua xyoo ntshab nuav. Thov caw mej paab kuv ua kuam xyoo nuav yog ib xyoo lom zem hab vaam meej rua mej tug miv nyuas. Luas tshawb ntshav tau tas tug miv nyuas kws muaj kev paab nyob rua tom tsev rua kev nyeem ntawv hab kev kawm ntawv nua mas kawm tau zoo dlua le ib tug kws tsi muaj kev paab nyob rua tom tsev. Yuav kuam tej tsev kawm ntawv zoo mas cov nais khu hab cov nam txiv yuav tsum lug koom teg.

Ib yaam kws kuv yuav thov kuam mej ua yog kuam mej qha kuv txug mej tug miv nyuas kuam kuv paub nwg zoo ntxiv. Tes xyoo nuav, kuv yuav xaa ntawv rua mej qha txug tej yaam kws mej hab mej tug miv nyuas yuav muaj cuab kaav lug ua tau ua ke rua tom tsev. Tej yaam ntawd yuav paab mej tug miv nyuas rua tej yaam kws peb yuav kawm nyob rua huv tsev kawm ntawv. Thov ua tej ntawd les kws ua tau. (Tej kws kuv yuav xaa rua mej yuav yog ua lug aaskiv. Yog mej xaav kuam kuv muab txhais ua mej cov lug, thov sau npe rua huv qaab hab muab xaa tuaj rua tsev kawm ntawv. Kuv le maam yos ib tug nais khu kws has tau mej cov lug los yog ib tug kws yuav lug paab tau mej.)

Ob yaam tseem ceeb tshaaj nplawg kws mej muaj cuab kaav yuav lug ua tau paab mej tug miv nyuas yog:

• **Nyeem hab thaam txug ntawv ua ke.** Mej muaj cuab kaav nyeem rua mej tug miv nyuas noog, mej tug miv nyuas nyeem rua mej noog, los mej nyeem ua ke los tau ib yaam.

• **Ua kuam mej tug miv nyuas pum mej nyeem hab sau ntawv.** Qhov nuav yuav qha tau rua mej tug miv nyuas tas mej xaav has tas kev nyeem ntawv yog ib yaam tseem ceeb hab lom zem heev. Ncu ntsoov, mej yuav nyeem ntawv aaskiv los mej cov lug los nyeem tau. Qhov tseem ceeb mas yog kuam mej tug miv nyua pum mej nyeem ntawv xwb.

Muaj ib qhov ntxiv kws kuv xaav thov kuam mej ua hab. Yog mej txawj lug aaskiv hab mej cov lug, thov qha rua kuv paub yog mej xaav paab lwm tsev tuab neeg kws has mej cov lug hab.

Ua tsaug kws mej tseem koom \rug kuv nyob rua mej tug miv nyuas kev kawm ntawv.

Sau npe,

_____

Yog ua tau, thov muab txhais ua kuv cov lug.
Kuv cov lug yog _____
Npe _____ Xuv tooj _____

親愛的家長：

歡迎各位！在這一新的學年中，我要求大家幫助我使它成爲對你（們）孩子來講是一個令人鼓舞和成功的一年。研究表明，如果孩子們的讀書和學習得到家庭支持的話，他們就能在學校中學習得更好一些。爲了使各類學校取得成功，家庭和教師必需共同努力。

我要求你（們）做的一件事是提供給我使我能更多地瞭解你(們)孩子的各種信息。整個學年中，我會發送一些你（們）可和孩子可以一起做的家庭活動的設想給你（們）。這些活動對你（們）的孩子在校中的學習會有所幫助。請盡可能多參加這些活動。(我送來的材料是用用英文寫的，如需要將它們譯成你（們）本國語言，請墊寫下面的表格並送回學校。我會安排雙語教師或其他助手來協助你（們）。)

在所有你（們）能在家中幫助孩子做的事情中，有兩件是特別重要的：

·和你(們)的孩子一起讀書，一起討論。你（們）可讀給孩子聽，也可讓孩子讀給你（們）聽，或者一起讀。和孩子一同上圖書館。這樣你們可挑選共同感興趣的書籍。這些圖書可以是用英文寫的，也可以是用你（們）本國語言寫的。

·讓你（們）的孩子看你（們）讀書。這會告訴你（們）的孩子，你(們)認爲讀書是有用和有趣的。不論你（們）讀的是英文或者是你（們）的本國語言是無關緊要的。對你（們）孩子來講，最重要的是要看到你（們）在讀書。

我還有一個特別的請求，如果你（們）通撓英文和本國兩種語言並願意協助其他講你（們）國家語言的家庭的話，請告訴我。

眞誠的，

_____

如果可能，請安排人爲我翻譯這些材料。
我的本國語言是 _____

សូមជូនចំពោះ មាតាបិតា,

សូមស្វាគមន៍...ដល់ឆ្នាំសិក្សាថ្មី។

ខ្ញុំសូមរពឹញលោកអ្នកអោយជួយធ្វើឆ្នាំសិក្សានេះជាឆ្នាំសិក្សាដ៏រីរួយចិត្តហើយនិងជោគ ជ័យដល់កូនលោកអ្នក។ ការសិក្សាស្រាវជ្រាវបានបង្ហាញអោយឃើញថា កូនក្នុងណាដែលមានការជួយខ្នះម្មក្នុងការអាន អក្សរហើយបាត់រៀននៅផ្ទះ រៀនពូកែនៅសាលារៀន។ ដើម្បីអោយសាលារៀនបានជោគជ័យ មាតាបិតានិងគ្រូច្រៀនដាច់ ខាតត្រូវមានសាមគ្គីភាពនិងគ្នា។

វត្តមួយដែលខ្ញុំ និងសូរលោកអ្នកធ្វើ
គឺសុំអោយលោកអ្នកផ្ដល់ពត៌មានអ្វីៗដែលនិងអាចជួយខ្ញុំបានយល់ច្បាស់លាស់អំពីកូន របស់លោកអ្នក។ ពេញទាំងមួយឆ្នាំសិក្សានេះ ខ្ញុំនិងផ្ញើកិនិតសំរាប់លោកអ្នកអំកិនិកូនរាចធ្វើសកម្មភាពជាមួយនិងកូននៅផ្ទះ។ សកម្មភាពទាំងអស់នេះនិងជួយកូនលោកអ្នកនៅអ្វីដែលបើងកំពុងគេសិក្សានៅសាលារៀន។ សូមលោកអ្នកចូលរួមក្នុង ការសិក្សានេះអោយបានច្រើនដែលលោកអ្នកអាចធ្វើទៅបាន។ (សម្មារដែលខ្ញុំ និងផ្ញើរទៅផ្ទះ គឺជាសម្មារជាភាសាអង់គ្លេស
បើសិនជាលោកអ្នកត្រូវការសម្មារនេះបកប្រែទៅជាភាសាដើមរបស់លោកអ្នក សូមបំពេញក្រដាសខាងក្រោម ហើយផ្ញើរ ត្រឡប់មកសាលាវិញ។ ខ្ញុំនិងខិតខំរៀបចំរកគ្រូបច្រៀនដែលចេះពីរភាសា ឬ អ្នកជំនួយជួយលោកអ្នក។

វត្តមួយដែលលោកអ្នកអាចធ្វើដើម្បីជួយកូនលោកអ្នកនៅផ្ទះបាន មានវត្តសំខាន់ជាងគេពីរគឺ:
• **ចូររអានសៀ្យវអៅនិងដៃជ្រកដោះស្រាយជាមួយនិងកូន។** លោកអ្នកអាចអ៉ានអោយកូនស្ដាប់ រឹងកូនរបស់លោកអ្នករិញក៍ អាចអានឲ្យលោកអ្នកស្ដាប់ដែរ ឬ ក៍អានជាមួយគ្នា។ ចូររទៅបណ្ណាល័យជាមួយកូន ធ្វើដូច្នេះលោកអ្នកអាចជ្រើសរើសសៀ្យវ អៅដែលលោកអ្នកនិងកូនចូលចិត្តអាន។
សៀ្យវអៅដែលលោកអ្នកអានអាចជាសៀ្យវអៅសរសេរជាភាសាអង់គ្លេស ឬ ក៍ជា ភាសាដើមរបស់លោកអ្នក។

• **ចូរធ្វើអោយកូនឃើញលោកអ្នកអានសៀ្យវអៅ។** ធ្វើដូច្នេះលោកអ្នកបង្ហាញកូនថា ការអានអក្សរ គឺវ៉ាមានតម្លៃណាស់និង សប្បាយទៀតផង។ មួងទៀត
ទោះជាលោកអ្នកអានអក្សរជាភាសាដើមរបស់លោកអ្នក ឬ ក៍ក្នុងភាសាអង់គ្លេសក៍ដោយ គឺវ៉ាមិនសំខាន់ទេ។ ការត្រានតែមើលឃើញលោកអ្នកអាន គឺវ៉ាសំខាន់ណាស់ដល់កូនរបស់លោកអ្នក។

ខ្ញុំមានការស្នើសុំពិសេសសម្មួយ។ បើសិនជាលោកអ្នកចេះពីរភាសា
គឺភាសាដើមរបស់លោកអ្នកនិងភាសាអង់គ្លេស សូមប្រាប់ អោយខ្ញុំបាននឹងផង
បើសិនជាលោកអ្នកមានចិត្តចង់ជួយដល់ក្រុមគ្រួសារផ្សេងទៀត ដែលចេះភាសារបស់លោកអ្នក។

សូមអរគុណចំពោះការយកចិត្តទុកដាក់ធ្វើការជាមួយនិងខ្ញុំ ដើម្បីការសិក្សារបស់កូនលោកអ្នក។

ហត្ថលេខា

_____

បើសិនជាអាចធ្វើទៅបាន ចូររអ្នកករណាម្នាក់ជួយបកប្រសម្មារសិក្សានេះអោយខ្ញុំផង។
ភាសាដើមរបស់ខ្ញុំគឺ _____
ឈ្មោះ: _____ លេខតេលេហ្នុ _____

Student Inventory

Please complete the information below with your child. It will help all of us to work together more effectively. Please return the form by _____.

Child's Name _____

Person Providing This Information _____

Relationship to Child _____

Has the child attended other schools? _____ Where? _____

_____

Number of Brothers _____ Ages _____

Number of Sisters _____ Ages _____

Other Family Members Living at Home _____

_____

_____

_____

Languages Spoken at Home _____

Child's Hobbies _____

_____

Reading Interests _____

_____

_____

_____

_____

Other Interests _____

_____

_____

Things my child does well: _____

_____

What I would like my child to accomplish this year: _____

_____

_____

_____

Please use the back of this form for any additional information.

Información sobre el estudiante

Este formulario nos ayudará a hacer un trabajo más eficaz. Por favor, complételo con su niño/a y envíelo a la escuela antes del _____.

Nombre del estudiante _____

Persona que proporciona la información _____

Relación con el estudiante _____

¿Ha asistido el estudiante a otras escuelas?_____ ¿Cuáles? _____
_____

Cantidad de hermanos _____ Edad _____

Cantidad de hermanas _____ Edad _____

Otros familiares que viven en la misma casa _____
_____
_____

Idiomas que hablan en el hogar _____

Pasatiempos preferidos del estudiante _____
_____

Tipos de lectura preferidos _____
_____
_____
_____
_____
_____

Otros intereses _____
_____
_____

Cosas que el estudiante hace bien: _____
_____

Me gustaría que mi niño/a logre lo siguiente este año: _____
_____
_____
_____

Si desea añadir algo más, por favor escríbalo en la parte de atrás de esta hoja.

Oink, Oink, Oink

Dear Family,

For the next few weeks, we'll be enjoying a theme entitled "Oink, Oink, Oink." We will be reading three different versions of "The Three Little Pigs."

Theme-related Activities to Do Together

It's Raining Cats and Dogs!

Invite your child to find humor in expressions that can be interpreted in more than one way. How might you draw someone "making a pig of himself or herself"? a salad dressing? time flying? running shoes? Ask your child to find similar expressions and draw pictures of each.

Sharing TV Humor

Watch a TV show with your child that both of you consider funny. Talk about what makes the show humorous. Think about similar shows that are not quite as much fun. What makes this show special?

Recycling Old Jokes

Tell your child a joke that was popular when you were a youngster. Invite the child to collect similar jokes from relatives, family friends, and neighbors. Which are still told today? Which are told with slight variations?

Theme-related Books to Enjoy Together

★ = Multicultural

Hamlet and the Enormous Chinese Dragon Kite by Brian Lies. Houghton 1995 (32p) Ignoring warnings from his friends, Hamlet the pig decides to fly a huge kite.

Jig, Fig, and Mrs. Pig by Peter Hansard. Candlewick 1995 (28p) In this variant of a Perrault fairy tale, a young pig is punished for his rudeness, and a hardworking servant is rewarded.

★ *Mufaro's Beautiful Daughters* by John Steptoe. Lothrop 1987 (32p) In this Zimbabwean Cinderella story, the king must choose one of Mufaro's daughters. All characters' names are from the Shona language.

Pigs Ahoy by David McPhail. Dutton 1995 (28p) The zany adventures of pigs at sea.

Three Cool Kids by Rebecca Emberley. Little, Brown 1995 (32p) A witty, urban slant on the tale of "The Three Billy Goats Gruff."

Tommy at the Grocery Store by Bill Grossman. HarperCollins 1989 (32p) In a visit to the grocery store, Tommy is mistaken for a salami and other edible items.

➡ Visit the library for books you can read together.

Parenting Tip

Your child may have discovered that humor can make a bad situation better. Help him or her also learn that teasing only makes a bad situation worse. Role-play appropriate responses to uncomfortable situations. For example, your child might consider how a smile might help a newcomer feel more at ease.

Cuentacolitas

Queridos familiares:

Las siguientes semanas, trataremos el tema "Cuentacolitas". Leeremos tres versiones distintas de "Los tres cerditos".

Actividades para hacer con su niño/a

¡Llueven sapos y culebras!

Animen a su niño/a a que se dé cuenta del humor que contienen las expresiones que tienen varias interpretaciones. ¿Cómo se puede dibujar a alguien que "come como un cerdo"? ¿Al tiempo que vuela? Pídanle a su niño/a que diga expresiones similares y que las dibuje.

Compartir el humor de la televisión

Miren un programa de televisión con su niño/a que a todos les parezca gracioso. Hablen de lo que hace al programa gracioso. Piensen en programas similares que no son tan graciosos. ¿Qué lo hace a éste especial?

Reciclaje de viejos chistes

Cuéntenle a su niño/a un cuento que se contaba cuando ustedes eran niños. Anime a su niño/a a que averigüe chistes similares de familiares, amigos de la familia y vecinos. ¿Cuáles se cuentan aún? ¿Cuáles se cuentan con variaciones?

Libros con que su niño/a puede disfrutar

Hamlet and the Enormous Chinese Dragon Kite por Brian Lies. Houghton 1995 (32p) Hamlet, el cerdo, ignora los consejos de los amigos y decide volar en una enorme cometa.

Jig, Fig, and Mrs. Pig por Peter Hansard. Candlewick 1995 (28p) En esta versión de un cuento de hadas de Perrault, a un joven cerdito lo castigan por sus malos modales, y recompensan a un sirviente que trabaja duro.

★ ***Mufaro's Beautiful Daughters*** por John Steptoe. Lothrop 1987 (32p) En este cuento de Cenicienta zimbabwense, el rey debe escoger a una de las hijas de Mufaro. Los nombres de todos los personajes están tomados de la lengua shona.

Pigs Ahoy por David McPhail. Dutton 1995 (28p) Las aventuras de unos cerdos en el mar.

Three Cool Kids por Rebecca Emberley. Little, Brown 1995 (32p) Una versión simpática y urbana del cuento "Three Billy Goats Gruff."

Tommy at the Grocery Store por Bill Grossman. HarperCollins 1989 (32p) Cuando Tommy visita una tienda de comestibles, lo confunden con un salame y otras comidas.

★ = Multicultural

➡ **Visiten la biblioteca y busquen libros para leer juntos.**

Consejo para los padres

Su hijo/a tal vez haya descubierto que el buen humor es capaz de mejorar una mala situación. Ayúdelo/la a comprender que cuando uno le hace bromas a alguien, se empeora la situación. Asuman papeles con las respuestas apropiadas para situaciones incómodas. Por ejemplo, pueden considerar cómo una sonrisa puede ayudar a un recién llegado a sentirse cómodo.

NEWSLETTER

Community Ties

Dear Family,

For the next few weeks, we'll be enjoying the theme "Community Ties." We will be reading about urban and rural communities. We will explore the ways people in communities work together to make their neighborhood a better place to live.

Theme-related Activities to Do Together

Neighborhood Links

Invite your child to choose a community function that the family can participate in. It might be a cleanup project on your street, a fundraiser, or an outing for a club or volunteer group.

Links in a Chain

Encourage your child to count all of the ways your family is linked to the larger community. Be sure to include not only water, gas, and electricity, but also communication links like cable TV, computer modems, telephone lines, and postal service.

Comparing Communities

Suggest that your child write a letter describing your community to a friend or relative in another community. Ask the pen pal to describe his or her community. How are they alike? How are they different?

Theme-related Books to Enjoy Together

★ *At the Crossroads* by Rachel Isadora. Greenwillow 1991 (32p) A group of South African children await their fathers' return after ten months of working in the mines.

How to Get Famous in Brooklyn by Amy Hest. Simon 1995 (32p) Janie has a notebook in which she records her observations as she walks through her neighborhood.

★ *Kimako's Story* by June Jordan. Houghton 1981 (48p) A little girl describes her everyday life in the city.

★ *Kodomo: A Visit with Japanese Children* by Susan Kuklin. Putnam 1995 (48p) This photo essay explores the everyday lives of contemporary Japanese children.

Once Around the Block by Kevin Henkes. Greenwillow 1987 (24p) Annie, bored while waiting for her father to come home from work, takes a walk around the block.

Ox-Cart Man by Donald Hall. Viking 1979 (40p) This selection shows day-to-day life through the changing seasons in an early New England village.

★ *A Picture Book of Martin Luther King, Jr.* by David A. Adler. Holiday 1989 (32p) The life and works of Dr. King are detailed in simple text.

★ = Multicultural

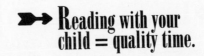

Reading with your child = quality time.

Parenting Tip

Set aside ten or fifteen minutes each day to read aloud to your child. Take turns choosing books. Discuss what made a particular book enjoyable and another a bore.

Nuestra comunidad

Queridos familiares:

Las siguientes semanas, trataremos el tema "Nuestra comunidad". Leeremos sobre comunidades rurales y urbanas. Exploraremos las formas en que las personas en las comunidades trabajan en conjunto y hacen que su vecindario sea un lugar mejor para vivir.

Actividades para hacer con su niño/a

Lazos en el vecindario

Animen a su niño/a a escoger una función de la comunidad en la cual la familia puede participar. Puede ser un proyecto para limpiar la calle, una recaudación de fondos o una excursión de un club o grupo de voluntarios.

Eslabones de una cadena

Pídanle a su niño/a que cuente todas las maneras en que la familia está ligada a la comunidad. Asegúrense de incluir no sólo el agua, el gas y la electricidad, sino también los lazos de comunicación tales como la TV de cable, los modems de computadoras, las líneas telefónicas y el servicio postal.

Comparación de comunidades

Sugiéranle a su niño/a que escriba una carta que le describa su comunidad a una amistad o un familiar que vive en otra comunidad. Pídanle a esa persona que describa su comunidad. ¿En qué se parecen? ¿En qué se diferencian?

Libros con que su niño/a puede disfrutar

★ *At the Crossroads* por Rachel Isadora. Greenwillow 1991 (32p) Un grupo de niños sudafricanos esperan que sus padres regresen después de trabajar por diez meses en las minas.

How to Get Famous in Brooklyn por Amy Hest. Simon 1995 (32p) Janie tiene un cuaderno en el que anota sus observaciones mientras camina por su vecindario.

★ *Kimako's Story* por June Jordan. Houghton 1981 (48p) Una niñita describe su vida cotidiana en la ciudad.

★ *Kodomo: A Visit with Japanese Children* por Susan Kuklin. Putnam 1995 (48p) Este ensayo fotográfico explora la vida cotidiana de los niños japoneses de la actualidad.

Once Around the Block por Kevin Henkes. Greenwillow 1987 (24p) Annie, cansada de esperar que su padre vuelva del trabajo, da una vuelta a la cuadra.

Ox-Cart Man por Donald Hall. Viking 1979 (40p) Esta selección muestra la vida diaria de hace tiempo, a través de las estaciones del año, en un pueblo de Nueva Inglaterra.

★ *A Picture Book of Martin Luther King, Jr.* por David A. Adler. Holiday 1989 (32p) La vida y las obras del Dr. King aparecen detallados en forma simple.

★ = Multicultural

➡ Leer con su niño/a = momentos preciados.

Consejo para los padres

Reserven diez o quince minutos diarios para leerle a su niño/a. Túrnense con su niño/a para escoger los libros. Hablen de qué hizo que un libro fuera interesante y otro aburrido.

DISASTER!

Dear Family,

For the next few weeks, we'll be exploring the theme "Disaster!" As we read about sinking ships, exploding volcanoes, and bursting storage tanks, your child will learn about acts of courage and caring. We will also discover how people respond to disasters.

Theme-related Activities to Do Together

Helping Out

Discuss groups that help people in trouble. Your child can learn about the Salvation Army, the Red Cross, and local groups that provide food in emergencies or run programs at hospitals. You may ask your child to contribute to one of these groups by donating a toy, clothing, a book, or canned goods.

Home Safety

As a family project, check your house for hazards. Call your local fire station and ask for information about the best way to store household chemicals and other potential hazards. Check to make sure that your smoke detectors are working.

Reporting on Disasters

Encourage your child to research a disaster that occurred long ago. Possible topics include the Great Chicago Fire or the *Hindenburg*. Ask your child to report on what he or she learned by doing what good reporters do. Their stories always answer these questions: Who? What? Where? When? Why? How?

Theme-related Books to Enjoy Together

★ = Multicultural

Crossing the New Bridge by Emily Arnold McCully. Putnam 1984 (32p) The mayor seeks the happiest person in town to be the first to cross the New Bridge and thus keep disaster from striking.

Discovering Earthquakes and Volcanoes by Laura Damon. Troll 1990 (32p) This nonfiction selection describes the causes of earthquakes and volcanoes and explains where they are most likely to occur.

★ *The Emperor's Garden* by Ferida Wolff. Tambourine 1994 (32p) Monsoon rains destroy the garden that villagers made to honor the Supreme Emperor of All China.

Powerful Waves by D. M. Souza. Carolrhoda 1992 (32p) This nonfiction selection explains how tidal waves, also called "tsunamis," are formed.

The Washout by Carol Carrick. Clarion 1978 (32p) When a sudden storm washes out the road, Christopher and his dog are caught in an exciting adventure.

➤ **Read together!**

Parenting Tip

Keep a list of emergency numbers near every telephone in the house. Discuss each number with your child. Role-play which number or numbers to call in an emergency and what information to provide.

¡DESASTRE!

Queridos familiares:

Las siguientes semanas, trataremos el tema "¡Desastre!". A medida que leamos acerca de barcos que se hunden y volcanes y tanques que explotan, su niño/a aprenderá qué son los actos de arrojo y de compasión. También descubriremos cómo las personas reacciona ante los desastres.

Actividades para hacer con su niño/a

Ayudar

Hablen de grupos que ayudan a las personas con dificultades. Su niño/a puede aprender qué es el Ejército de Salvación, la Cruz Roja y los grupos locales que proveen comida durante emergencias o que tienen programas en los hospitales. Tal vez deseen que su niño/a contribuya a uno de estos grupos mediante la donación de un juguete, ropa, un libro o comidas.

Seguridad casera

Lleven a cabo la tarea familiar de revisar la casa y asegurarse de que no haya peligros. Llamen a la oficina de los bomberos y pregunten cuál es la manera de guardar químicos caseros y otras cosas que sean peligros en potencia. Asegúrense de que los detectores de incendios funcionan.

Anunciar un desastre

Animen a su niño/a a que averigüe datos sobre un desastre que ocurrió hace mucho tiempo. Ejemplos de temas son el Gran Incendio de Chicago o el *Hindenburg*. Pídanle que informe lo que aprendió de la manera que lo haría un buen reportero. Los informes de los reporteros contestan las siguientes preguntas: ¿de quién? ¿qué? ¿dónde? ¿cuándo? ¿por qué? ¿cómo?

Libros con que su niño/a puede disfrutar

★ = Multicultural

Crossing the New Bridge por Emily Arnold McCully. Putnam 1984 (32p) El alcalde busca la persona más feliz de la ciudad para que ésta cruce el Puente Nuevo y prevenga desastres.

Discovering Earthquakes and Volcanoes por Laura Damon. Troll 1990 (32p) Esta selección de hechos de la vida real describe las causas de los terremotos y volcanes y explica dónde es más posible que ocurran.

★ *The Emperor's Garden* por Ferida Wolff. Tambourine 1994 (32p) Las lluvias del monzón destruyen el jardín que los habitantes del pueblo hicieron para rendir honores al Emperador de la China.

Powerful Waves por D. M. Souza. Carolrhoda 1992 (32p) Esta selección explica cómo se forman las olas gigantescas, también llamadas "tsunamis".

The Washout por Carol Carrick. Clarion 1978 (32p) Christopher y su perro viven una aventura cuando una tormenta repentina borra el camino por el que iban.

➡➡ ¡Lean juntos!

Consejo para los padres

Tengan una lista de los números de emergencia cerca de cada teléfono de la casa. Hablen de cada número con su niño/a. Asuman papeles sobre qué número llamar en una emergencia y qué datos dar.

NEWSLETTER

Dear Family,

For the next few weeks, we'll be exploring a theme entitled "What's Cooking?" Your child will read stories that center around foods enjoyed in countries around the world.

Theme-related Activities to Do Together

Kitchen Math

Help your child answer the following questions: How many thirds of a cup equal two cups? How many fourths of a cup equal two cups? How many teaspoons are in one tablespoon?

Rating Recipes

Select three favorite recipes. Ask your child to compare the recipes. How are they alike? How is each different? You may wish to test each recipe and then ask the child to rate it. Which tastes best? What ingredient made the difference?

Brewing Sun Tea

On a warm day, invite your child to try solar cooking. Pour water into a jar, add herbal tea bags, and then put a lid on the jar. After the jar has sat in the sun for three or four hours, you will have sun-brewed tea.

Theme-related Books to Enjoy Together

★ *Aunt Flossie's Hats (And Crab Cakes Later)* by Elizabeth Fitzgerald Howard. Clarion 1991 (32p) Sarah and Susan's visits to Great-Aunt Flossie in Maryland end with delicious crab cakes.

★ *Carlos and the Cornfield/ Carlos y la milpa de maíz* by Jan Romero Stevens. Northland 1995 (32p) In his haste to finish the task, Carlos drops too many corn seeds in each row.

★ *Corn Is Maize: The Gift of the Indians* by Aliki. HarperCollins 1976 (40p) This nonfiction selection explains how corn was found by Indian farmers hundreds of years ago.

★ *Market Days* by Madhur Jaffrey. BridgeWater 1995 (32p) A tour of marketplaces around the world, including Italy, China, Senegal, Egypt, India, and Mexico.

Olga's Cup and Saucer: A Picture Book with Recipes by Olga Bravo. Holt 1995 (32p) The owner of a famous bakery tells how Nickel Penny becomes a baker. Some of Penny's recipes are included.

Thunder Cake by Patricia Polacco. Philomel 1990 (32p) Baking a thunder cake with her grandmother helps a young girl overcome her fear of storms.

★ *The Tortilla Factory* by Gary Paulsen. Harcourt 1995 (32p) From seed to factory to store, Paulsen tells how tortillas are made.

★ = Multicultural

➤ **Start a family tradition— read together.**

Parenting Tip

Invite your child to assist you in the kitchen by taking charge of the measuring. Help the child to discover how many teaspoons a quarter cup contains. As you cook, discuss how heating or cooling a liquid changes its appearance. Or experiment with recipes by adding more or less of an ingredient.

¡Buen provecho!

Queridos familiares:

Las siguientes semanas, trataremos el tema "¡Buen provecho!". Su niño/a leerá relatos sobre comidas que se disfrutan en distintas partes del mundo.

Actividades para hacer con su niño/a

Matemáticas en la cocina

Ayuden a su niño/a a contestar las siguientes preguntas: ¿Cuántos tercios de taza son iguales a dos tazas? ¿Cuántos cuartos de taza son iguales a dos tazas? ¿Cuántas cucharaditas hay en una cuchara sopera?

Evaluar recetas

Seleccionen tres recetas preferidas. Pídanle a su niño/a que compare las recetas. ¿En qué se parecen? ¿En qué es diferente cada una? Tal vez quieran probar cada preparación y pedirle a su niño/a que las evalúe. ¿Cuál sabe mejor? ¿Qué ingrediente la hace mejor?

Preparar té de sol

Un día caluroso, animen a su niño/a a que cocine con el calor del sol. Pongan agua en un recipiente, agreguen bolsitas de té de hierbas y pongan una tapa en el recipiente. Después de que éste esté en el sol unas tres o cuatro horas, tendrán té de sol.

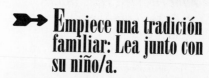

Libros con que su niño/a puede disfrutar

★ **Aunt Flossie's Hats (And Crab Cakes Later)** por Elizabeth Fitzgerald Howard. Clarion 1991 (32p) Las visitas de Sarah y Susan a la tía-abuela Flossie que vive en Maryland culminan con deliciosos patelillos de cangrejo.

★ **Carlos and the Cornfield/ Carlos y la milpa de maíz** por Jan Romero Stevens. Northland 1995 (32p) Por apurarse para acabar su tarea, Carlos echa demasiadas semillas de maíz en cada hilera. El texto está en español e inglés.

★ **Corn Is Maize: The Gift of the Indians** por Aliki. HarperCollins 1976 (40p) Esta selección de relatos de la vida real explica cómo los agricultores indios descubrieron el maíz hace cientos de años.

★ **Market Days** por Madhur Jaffrey. BridgeWater 1995 (32p) Un viaje por los mercados del mundo, incluso Italia, China, Senegal, Egipto, India y México.

Olga's Cup and Saucer: A Picture Book with Recipes por Olga Bravo. Holt 1995 (32p) El dueño de una panadería famosa cuenta cómo Nickel Penny aprende a hacer pan. Tiene algunas de las recetas de Penny.

Thunder Cake por Patricia Polacco. Philomel 1990 (32p) Una niñita se sobrepone a su miedo a las tormentas cuando hace un pastel de truenos con su abuela.

★ **La tortillería** por Gary Paulsen. Harcourt 1995 (32p) De la semilla a la fábrica a la tienda, Paulsen cuenta cómo se hacen las tortillas.

★ = Multicultural

➡ **Empiece una tradición familiar: Lea junto con su niño/a.**

Consejo para los padres

Pídanle a su niño/a que ayude en la cocina encargándose de las medidas. Hagan que su niño/a descubra cuántas cucharaditas hay en un cuarto de taza. Mientras cocinan, hablen de cómo cambia la apariencia de un líquido cuando se calienta o se enfría. O experimenten con recetas agregando más o menos de un ingrediente.

Weather Watch

Dear Family,

For the next few weeks, we'll be exploring a theme entitled "Weather Watch." Your child will read stories about tornadoes, thunderstorms, and snowstorms. We will also conduct some weather-related experiments.

Theme-related Activities to Do Together

Predicting the Weather

Encourage your child to notice signs of a change in the weather. Have clouds covered the sun? Did the wind abruptly change speed or direction? Has the temperature dropped suddenly? Speculate as to what these changes might mean in terms of tomorrow's weather. Invite your child to test his or her ideas.

In Case of Emergency

Discuss with your child the kinds of weather-related emergencies common in your area and how to prepare for them. For example, do you have candles, flashlights, and a transistor radio in case the power goes out? Where is the safest place in your home during a tornado or a hurricane? Do you have a list of phone numbers to call in a weather-related emergency?

Is It True What They Say?

"Rain before seven. Over by eleven." "Evening red and morning gray. Two sure signs of one fine day." Are these and other weather-related sayings true? Invite your child to test them. If your child seems interested, suggest that he or she collect other such sayings.

Theme-related Books to Enjoy Together

Before the Storm by Jane Yolen. Boyds Mills 1995 (32p) The author describes the feeling of a hot summer day just before a storm.

Dark Cloud, Strong Breeze by Susan Patron. Orchard 1994 (32p) A young girl and her father have locked their keys in the car, and a storm is fast approaching.

Dear Rebecca, Winter Is Here by Jean Craighead George. HarperCollins 1993 (32p) A grandmother writes a letter to her granddaughter on December 21, the winter solstice.

How's the Weather? A Look at Weather and How It Changes by Melvin Berger and Gilda Berger. Hambleton-Hill 1993 (32p) Clearly illustrated explanations of what causes weather to change.

The Magic School Bus Inside a Hurricane by Joanna Cole. Scholastic 1995 (32p) Ms. Frizzle and her class are off on another adventure.

★ ***The Orphan Boy*** by Tololwa Mollel. Clarion 1991 (32p) This East African tale explains why the planet Venus is known as Kileken to the Masai.

What Will the Weather Be? by Linda Dewitt. HarperCollins 1991 (32p) This nonfiction selection explains how meteorologists record and analyze data to make weather predictions.

★ = Multicultural

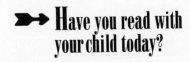
Have you read with your child today?

Parenting Tip

Invite your child to listen to the daily weather report. Have your child use that information to plan what he or she will wear the next day. This is a good way to encourage taking responsibility and avoiding angry words or tears over whether the child will need boots or a jacket.

¿Qué tiempo hace?

Queridos familiares:

Las siguientes semanas, trataremos el tema "¿Qué tiempo hace?". Su niño/a leerá cuentos acerca de tornados, tormentas eléctricas y de nieve. También haremos algunos experimentos relacionados con el tiempo.

Actividades para hacer con su niño/a

Predicción del tiempo

Animen a su niño/a a darse cuenta de los cambios del tiempo. ¿Se ha cubierto de nubes el sol? ¿Cambió de repente la dirección del viento? ¿Bajó de repente la temperatura? Predigan lo que significan los cambios para el tiempo de mañana. Pídanle a su niño/a que compruebe sus ideas.

En caso de emergencia

Hablen de las emergencias relacionadas con el tiempo que son comunes en la zona donde viven y de cómo prepararse en caso de emergencia. Por ejemplo, ¿tienen velas, linternas o un radio de pilas en caso de que se vaya la electricidad? ¿Cuál es el lugar más seguro en caso de que haya un tornado o huracán? ¿Tienen una lista de números a los cuales llamar en caso de emergencia?

¿Es cierto lo que cuentan?

"La lluvia temprana, se acaba a media mañana". "Atardecer rojo y mañana gris, día radiante quieren decir". ¿Son ciertos éstos y otros dichos relacionados con el tiempo? Si a su niño/a le interesa, pídanle que junte otros dichos similares.

Libros con que su niño/a puede disfrutar

Before the Storm por Jane Yolen. Boyds Mills 1995 (32p) La autora describe la sensación de un día caluroso de verano antes de que comience una tormenta.

Dark Cloud, Strong Breeze por Susan Patron. Orchard 1994 (32p) Una niña y su padre se dejaron las llaves dentro del carro y se aproxima una tormenta.

Dear Rebecca, Winter Is Here por Jean Craighead George. HarperCollins 1993 (32p) Una abuela escribe una carta a su nieta el 21 de diciembre, día del solsticio de invierno.

How's the Weather? A Look at Weather and How It Changes por Melvin Berger y Gilda Berger. Hambleton-Hill 1993 (32p) Explicaciones ilustradas acerca de lo que hace que cambie el tiempo.

The Magic School Bus Inside a Hurricane por Joanna Cole. Scholastic 1995 (32p) La Sra. Frizzle y su clase emprenden una nueva aventura.

★ **The Orphan Boy** por Tololwa Mollel. Clarion 1991 (32p) Esta historia del este de África explica por qué los maasai conocen el planeta Venus por el nombre de Kileken.

What Will the Weather Be? por Linda Dewitt. HarperCollins 1991 (32p) Esta selección de la vida real explica cómo los meteorólogos anotan y analizan datos para hacer las predicciones del tiempo.

★ = Multicultural

 ¿Ha leído con su niño/a hoy?

Consejo para los padres

Pídanle a su niño/a que escuche el informe del tiempo. Hagan que su niño/a use lo que escuchó para decidir qué ropa se va a poner al día siguiente. Ésta es una buena manera de desarrollar la responsabilidad y evitar enojos y lágrimas si su niño/a tiene que llevar botas o una chaqueta abrigada.

Dear Family,

For the next few weeks, we'll be enjoying a theme entitled "What a Day!" We will read stories about the day one child got a haircut and the day two others received a special surprise. We will also explore a factual account of a day in the life of a veterinarian.

Theme-related Activities to Do Together

What Kind of Day Was It?

At mealtime or after school, share the positive and negative aspects of the day with your child. Talk about your day and invite your child to share his or her experiences.

Keeping a Diary

A diary is a way of remembering activities, accomplishments, thoughts, hopes, and dreams. Invite your child to set aside a few minutes each evening to write about his or her day.

How Do They Celebrate?

Invite your child to explore how birthdays are celebrated around the world or the way children in other nations mark the last day of school. Your local library has a variety of books and videos about holidays and other celebrations in various cultures.

Theme-related Books to Enjoy Together ★ = Multicultural

Bea and Mr. Jones by Amy Schwartz. Bradbury 1982 (32p) Bea and her father trade jobs for the day. Bea goes to the office while her father goes to kindergarten.

★ **The Last Dragon** by Susan Miho Nunes. Clarion 1995 (32p) A faded, torn, silk dragon in a show window captures the attention and imagination of young Peter Chang, who decides to restore it.

★ **The Stories Julian Tells** by Ann Cameron. Knopf 1989 (96p) Julian's days are filled with adventures with his friend Gloria and brother Huey. See also *More Stories Julian Tells.*

Swim for Cover: Adventure on the Coral Reef by Sue Vyner. Crown 1995 (32p) An octopus swimming along the Great Barrier Reef barely escapes a pursuing moray eel.

★ **Tap-Tap** by Karen Lynn Williams. Clarion 1994 (34p) Sasifi is eager to take a ride in a tap-tap, a truck that carries passengers to market in rural Haiti.

What If It Never Stops Raining? by Nancy Carlson. Viking 1992 (32p) Family and friends help Tim, who worries about everything, get through the day.

➡ What you read doesn't matter, so long as you read together.

Parenting Tip

Decide with your child which household tasks will be the child's responsibility. Help your child find ways to remember the task. Also talk about how you and the child will decide if the job was well done.

Queridos familiares:

Las siguientes semanas, trataremos el tema "¡Qué día!". Leeremos relatos acerca del día en que un niño se cortó el cabello y otros dos niños recibieron una sorpresa. También exploraremos un testimonio verdadero de un día en la vida de un veterinario.

Actividades para hacer con su niño/a

¿Cómo fue el día?

A la hora de comer o después de la escuela, hablen de las cosas positivas y negativas que ocurrieron en el día. Hablen ustedes del día y pídanle a su niño/a que comparta sus propias experiencias.

Mantener un diario

Con un diario se pueden recordar actividades, logros, pensamientos, esperanzas y sueños. Animen a su niño/a a que reserve unos minutos todas las noches para escribir sobre lo que ocurrió en el día.

¿Cómo celebran?

Animen a su niño/a a que averigüe cómo se celebran los cumpleaños en otras partes del mundo o cómo los niños de otros países celebran el último día de clases. En la biblioteca más próxima hallarán una variedad de videos y libros sobre fiestas y celebraciones en varias culturas.

Libros con que su niño/a puede disfrutar ★ = Multicultural

Bea and Mr. Jones por Amy Schwartz. Bradbury 1982 (32p) Bea y su padre se intercambian los trabajos por un día. Bea va a la oficina mientras que su padre va al jardín de infantes.

★ **The Last Dragon** por Susan Miho Nunes. Clarion 1995 (32p) Un dragón de seda ya gastada que está en la vitrina de una tienda despierta la atención y la imaginación del joven Peter Chang, quien decide componerlo.

★ **The Stories Julian Tells** por Ann Cameron. Knopf 1989 (96p) La vida de Julián está llena de aventuras con su amiga Gloria y su hermano. Véase también *More Stories Julian Tells.*

Swim for Cover: Adventure on the Coral Reef por Sue Vyner. Crown 1995 (32p) Un pulpo que nada por el Gran Arrecife de coral se escapa de una anguila que lo persigue.

★ **Tap-Tap** por Karen Lynn Williams. Clarion 1994 (34p) Sasifi quiere dar una vuelta en un tap-tap, o camión que lleva pasajeros al mercado en la zona rural de Haití.

What If It Never Stops Raining? por Nancy Carlson. Viking 1992 (32p) La familia y los amigos ayudan a Tim, quien se preocupa por todo, a que pase el día.

➡ **No importa lo que lean, sino que lean juntos.**

Consejo para los padres

Decidan con su niño/a cuáles de las tareas de la casa serán su responsabilidad. Ayuden a su niño/a a que busque maneras de acordarse qué hacer. Hablen también acerca de cómo ustedes y su niño/a decidirán si la tarea se hizo correctamente.

Parent-Teacher Conferences

Request for Information

Soon I will be scheduling parent-teacher conferences. I thought I would check to see how we can arrange a conference that will best serve your needs. Please take a few moments to fill out the questionnaire below and return it to school by

_____.

I will do my best to accommodate any special needs you may have.

Your name: _____

Child's name: _____

Your relationship to the child: _____

Phone number: _____ Best time to reach you: _____

Check the time that would be best for you to come to school.
- ❏ before school
- ❏ morning
- ❏ during lunch
- ❏ afternoon
- ❏ after school
- ❏ evening
- ❏ weekend
- ❏ I can only participate in a conference by phone.

Check any item that would make it easier for you to attend the conference.
- ❏ child care available for other children
- ❏ translator
  language: _____
- ❏ transportation
- ❏ other: _____

❏ Please check here if you would be willing to serve as a translator for someone else.

Language(s): _____

Thank you for your response.

_____

Conferencias del maestro con los familiares

Pedido de información

Pronto comenzaré a organizar las conferencias con los padres. Quisiera saber qué sería lo más conveniente para usted. Le ruego que por favor complete este cuestionario y que lo envíe a la escuela el

_____.

Haré todo lo posible para tener en cuenta sus preferencias y necesidades.

Su nombre: _____

Nombre del estudiante: _____

Su relación con el estudiante: _____

Nº de teléfono: _____ Mejor hora para llamarlo/a: _____

Marque el momento que prefiere venir a la escuela.

❑ antes del inicio de las clases

❑ a la mañana

❑ durante el almuerzo

❑ a la tarde

❑ después de la escuela

❑ a la noche

❑ el fin de semana

❑ Sólo puedo participar en una conferencia que sea por teléfono.

Marque cualquier punto que facilitaría su asistencia a la conferencia.

❑ cuidado de niños

❑ traductor

idioma: _____

❑ transporte

❑ otros: _____

❑ Por favor, haga una marca si desea servir de traductor para otro.

Idioma(s): _____

Muchas gracias por responder a este cuestionario.

_____

Parent-Teacher Conference Outline

Student: _____ Conference date and time: _____

Family members attending conference: _____

_____

Student attending? ❏ Yes ❏ No

Share some of the materials in the Student's Evaluation Portfolio.
Identify beforehand specific items you want to share.

Ask parents to share how they think their child is doing. Discuss the reasons for their feelings.

_____

_____

Discuss the student's areas of strength. Identify beforehand specific examples to share with parents.

_____

_____

Discuss areas needing improvement. Identify beforehand specific examples to share with parents.

_____

_____

Share steps that will be taken in the classroom to help the student.

_____

_____

Suggest steps parents can take to help their child.

_____

_____

Suggest steps the student can take to make better progress.

_____

_____

Additional Notes _____

_____

_____

Post-Conference Action Plan

Student: _____

Date of conference: _____

Family members attending conference: _____

_____

_____

Goals (discussed in conference)

_____

_____

_____

Steps/Action to Take

Teacher: _____

_____

_____

_____

Parents: _____

_____

_____

_____

Student: _____

_____

_____

_____

Additional Notes

_____

_____

_____

Copy of Action Plan given to parents? ❏ Yes ❏ No

Parents and Teachers Working as Partners

Section Two of *Home/Community Connections* provides suggestions for helping parents become actively involved in activities that extend what their child is studying in the classroom. The materials include "family homework" and projects that parents can complete with their child, informational articles that inform and support parents on a variety of topics important to reading and education in general, forms that promote continued communication, and book and activity suggestions for extending learning at home during school breaks. Similar forms and information on the Teacher's Resource Disks are indicated with an icon.

❖ = Appears in English and Spanish

🖳 = Teacher's Resource Disks

TABLE OF CONTENTS FOR SECTION 2

Introduction ———————————————————————— **34**
    Getting Parents Actively Involved
    Maintaining Communication with Parents
    Related Reading

❖ **Family Homework**
    Oink, Oink, Oink ———————————————————— 35
    Community Ties ————————————————————— 37
    Disaster! ————————————————————————— 39
    What's Cooking? ————————————————————— 41
    Weather Watch ————————————————————— 43
    What a Day! ——————————————————————— 45

❖ **Home Projects**
    Oink, Oink, Oink. ————————————————————— 47
    Community Ties ————————————————————— 51
    Disaster! ————————————————————————— 55
    What's Cooking? ————————————————————— 59
    Weather Watch ————————————————————— 63
    What a Day! ——————————————————————— 67

❖ **Home Project Evaluation** ———————————————— **71**

❖ **Parent-Teacher-Child Dialogue** ————————————— **73**

❖ **Parent Articles**
    Help Your Child Become a Successful Reader ——————— 75
    The Writing Process ———————————————————— 77
    Handling Homework ———————————————————— 79
    Looking at Your Child's Progress ———————————— 81
    Guiding Your Child's TV Viewing ———————————— 83

🖳 ❖ **School's Out! (End-of-Year Books/Activities)** ————— **85**

Getting Parents Actively Involved

Family Homework The Family Homework sheet is sent home before the start of each new theme in class to describe the upcoming theme to parents and to provide a simple activity they can easily do with their child to activate interest and build background. Family Homework is provided in both English and Spanish, on pages 35–46.

Home Projects A project designed to extend the theme is available for each of the six themes in the program. These projects are to be completed by the child and a family member or friend. (Of course, it is important that children who complete the projects without the assistance of a family member not be penalized.) Home Projects have a place for you to indicate the date when the completed project should be brought to school. So that parents and children will know that their efforts are valued and appreciated, you may wish to display the projects, share them in class or with another class, or plan a celebration of some or all of the projects and invite family members to join in. Home Projects are provided in both English and Spanish on pages 47–72.

Parent Articles These articles inform and support parents by explaining what is known about topics important to parents, such as reading, writing, homework, and television viewing. They also suggest ways parents can help their child in these areas. Parent Articles are in English and Spanish on pages 75–84.

School's Out! (End-of-the-Year Books/Activities) This sheet provides activity and book suggestions for the summer or other school breaks. The books suggested for the child relate to reading themes to be studied during the next school year, and activities are listed both for the child to do alone and for the parent and child to do together. School's Out! is provided in English and Spanish on pages 85–86.

Maintaining Communication with Parents

Home Project Evaluation Form This form, which appears in both English and Spanish on pages 71–72, can be sent home with each Home Project. It will provide feedback from parents on whether they—and their child—enjoy the project and feel it was a worthwhile experience. This will help you assess the value of each project in your program.

Parent-Teacher-Child Dialogue Form This form (in English and Spanish, on pages 73–74) provides an easy way for teacher, parent, and child to maintain communication throughout the year. The form can be started by parent, teacher, or child at any time. You may find it helpful to make regular use of the form by sending it home at the end of each week, or by initiating it on an as-needed basis. Non-English-speaking families can communicate in their home language. You might use AT&T Language Line Service or a parent volunteer to translate their messages.

Related Reading

"Essential Elements of Strong Parent Involvement Programs," David L. Williams and Nancy Feyl Chavkin. *Educational Leadership*, October 1989, p. 18. The Southwest Educational Development Laboratory identifies seven essential elements of successful parent involvement programs.

Parents and Teachers: Helping Children Learn to Read and Write, Timothy V. Rasinski. Harcourt Brace, 1995. An expert in the field compiles timely articles by top educators on a great variety of subjects.

Strong Families, Strong Schools: Building Community Partnerships for Learning, U.S. Department of Education, September 1994. This national initiative encourages families to become actively involved in their children's learning, a critical factor in achieving high-quality education.

Family Homework

Soon we'll begin a new reading theme—"Oink, Oink, Oink." We'll read three very different versions of *The Three Little Pigs* and learn how an old story can be retold with a new twist. To help your child get ready, work together to invent a new version of a story your child already knows.

First, help your child identify a favorite story. You might look through books together or recall stories your child has been told by family members to help him or her decide on one.

Next, ask "what-if" questions about the story. For example: What if the story took place at the North Pole? What if the characters were real people instead of animals? Encourage your child to explore the possibilities.

Then help your child use some of these possibilities to make up a new story. Your child can write the title and a few sentences, telling what the new version is about, in the space below. Use the back of this paper for more writing space, if necessary.

_____

by _____

_____

_____

_____

_____

_____

_____

_____

Child's Name _____

Parent's Signature _____

Tareas escolares para la familia

Pronto vamos a comenzar con el nuevo tema de lectura llamado "Cuentacolitas". Leeremos tres versiones muy diferentes de *Los tres cerditos*. Aprenderemos que se puede cambiar un cuento tradicional agregándole algo nuevo. Para que su niño/a se familiarice con el tema, intercambien ideas para inventar una nueva versión de un cuento ya conocido.

Primero, ayude a su niño/a a seleccionar su cuento preferido. Para darle algunas ideas, podrían hojear libros o recordar relatos contados por miembros de la familia.

Luego, hágale preguntas sobre el cuento que empiecen con la frase "¿Qué pasaría si...? Podría comenzar con las siguientes: ¿Qué pasaría si el cuento sucediera en el Polo norte? ¿Qué pasaría si los personajes fueran personas en lugar de animales? Ayúdelo/la a explorar todas las posibilidades.

Luego, pídale que utilice algunas de esas alternativas para inventar una nueva versión del cuento. Dígale que escriba el título y un par de oraciones explicando de qué trata su versión del cuento. Puede escribir en el espacio de abajo y, si fuera necesario, continuar en el reverso de esta hoja.

por _____

_____

_____

_____

_____

_____

Nombre del/de la niño/a _____

Firma del padre, de la madre o del tutor _____

Family Homework

Soon we'll begin a new reading theme – "Community Ties." We'll learn how people within a community depend on one another. To help your child get ready, look for stories about local citizens, events, or issues in your newspaper.

First, help your child choose an article that sounds interesting. Read the article together. Then cut out the headline and tape or paste it in the space below.

Help your child write a few sentences, telling what the article is about. Encourage him or her to tell why the information is important.

Child's Name _____

Parent's Signature _____

Tareas escolares para la familia

Pronto vamos a comenzar con el nuevo tema de lectura llamado "Nuestra comunidad". Aprenderemos que las personas de una comunidad dependen las unas de las otras. Para que su niño/a se familiarice con el tema, busquen artículos en el periódico sobre ciudadanos, sucesos o problemas de la comunidad.

Primero, ayúdelo/la a elegir un artículo que parezca interesante. Léanlo juntos. Luego, dígale que recorte el titular y que lo pegue en el espacio en blanco de abajo.

Ayúdelo/la a escribir un par de oraciones para explicar de qué trata el artículo. Pídale que señale por qué ese artículo es importante.

Nombre del/de la niño/a _____

Firma del padre, de la madre o del tutor _____

Family Homework

Soon we'll begin a new reading theme—"Disaster!" We'll read about disasters in history, such as the sinking of the *Titanic* and the volcano that buried Pompeii, and their effect on the people who experienced them. To help your child get ready, invite him or her to interview you about a disaster you know about.

Encourage your child to ask you questions that begin with the words *who, what, when, where,* and *why.* Then have him or her write answers to the questions in the spaces below.

1. Who? _____

_____

2. What? _____

_____

3. When? _____

_____

4. Where? _____

_____

5. Why? _____

_____

Child's Name _____

Parent's Signature _____

Tareas escolares para la familia

Pronto vamos a comenzar con el nuevo tema de lectura llamado "¡Desastre!". Leeremos acerca de algunas calamidades famosas (como el naufragio del *Titanic* o la erupción del volcán que sepultó la ciudad de Pompeya), y sobre las consecuencias que sufrió la gente que las vivió. Para que su niño/a se familiarice con el tema, pídale que le haga una entrevista para averiguar la información que usted sepa acerca de alguna catástrofe.

Recuérdele que al hacer las preguntas comience con las palabras *quién, qué, cuándo, dónde* y *por qué*. A medida que usted vaya contestando, su niño/a puede escribir las respuestas en el espacio de abajo.

1. ¿Quién? _____

_____

2. ¿Qué? _____

_____

3. ¿Cuándo? _____

_____

4. ¿Dónde? _____

_____

5. ¿Por qué? _____

Nombre del/de la niño/a _____

Firma del padre, de la madre o del tutor _____

Family Homework

Soon we'll begin a new reading theme—"What's Cooking?" We'll learn about how people come together around food to share and celebrate. To help your child get ready, work together to select a favorite dish and write the recipe.

First, help your child choose a dish. It can be a personal favorite or a traditional family recipe. Or, you can look through a cookbook or magazine together to select a dish.

Help your child list the ingredients and write the steps of the recipe in order in the space below. (If the dish has a written recipe, you can read it together, and then your child can rewrite it in his or her own words. If the dish is a family recipe that's not written down, your child can ask you or another family member about the ingredients and steps.) Use the back of this paper for more writing space.

Dish: _____

Ingredients: _____

_____

_____

Steps: _____

_____

_____

_____

_____

_____

_____

_____

Child's Name _____

Parent's Signature _____

Tareas escolares para la familia

Pronto vamos a comenzar con el nuevo tema de lectura llamado "¡Buen provecho!". Aprenderemos que la gente se reúne alrededor de la comida para compartir y celebrar. Para que su niño/a se familiarice con el tema, escojan un plato que les guste a ambos y escriban la receta.

Primero, ayúdelo/la a elegir un plato. Puede ser un gusto personal o una comida tradicional de la familia. Otra posibilidad sería hojear una revista o un libro de cocina y seleccionar un plato.

Ayude a su niño/a a escribir la lista con los ingredientes y los pasos de la receta en el espacio en blanco de abajo. (Si tienen la receta por escrito, pueden leerla juntos, y luego su niño/a podrá escribirla usando sus propias palabras. Si se trata de una receta familiar y no la tienen por escrito, su niño/a puede preguntarle a usted o a otro pariente cuáles son los ingredientes y los pasos a seguir para preparar el plato.) Si le hace falta más espacio para escribir, puede usar el reverso de la hoja.

Plato: _____

Ingredientes: _____

_____

_____

Pasos: _____

_____

_____

_____

_____

_____

_____

Nombre del/de la niño/a _____

Firma del padre, de la madre o del tutor _____

Family Homework

Soon we'll begin a new reading theme—"Weather Watch." We'll learn about how changes in the weather can affect people's lives. To help your child get ready, read a weather report in a newspaper or watch one on TV. Then work together to write your own weather report.

First, talk about the weather report you read or watched.
- How are temperatures reported?
- What other information is included?
- What special symbols are used?
- What do you learn about today's weather? About tomorrow's?

Then help your child write a weather report in the space below.

Day of the Week: _____ Date: _____

Highest Temperature: _____

Lowest Temperature: _____

Type of Weather: _____

_____

_____

_____

_____

_____

_____

_____

Child's Name _____

Parent's Signature _____

Tareas escolares para la familia

Pronto vamos a comenzar con el nuevo tema de lectura llamado "¿Qué tiempo hace?" Aprenderemos sobre cómo pueden afectar los cambios atmosféricos a la vida de las personas. Para que su niño/a se familiarice con el tema, lean un reporte del tiempo en un periódico o mírenlo en la televisión. Luego, trabajen juntos para hacer su propio informe del tiempo.

Primero, platiquen acerca del reporte que leyeron en el periódico o miraron en la televisión.
- ¿Qué temperaturas fueron reportadas?
- ¿Qué otra información dieron?
- ¿Qué símbolos usaron?
- ¿Qué sabes acerca del tiempo del día de hoy? ¿Y del tiempo de mañana?

A continuación, ayude a su niño/a a escribir los datos para completar este reporte del tiempo.

Día de la semana: _____ Fecha: _____

Temperatura máxima: _____

Temperature mínima: _____

Tipo de condiciones atmosféricas: _____

_____

_____

_____

_____

Nombre del/de la niño/a _____

Firma del padre, de la madre o del tutor _____

Family Homework

Soon we'll begin a new reading theme—"What a Day!" We'll learn how each day of our lives is special in some way. To help your child get ready, help him or her to identify a special, unforgettable day.

Have your child draw a picture of what happened on that day. Then help your child write a paragraph about the day.

A Day I Will Never Forget

_____

_____

_____

_____

_____

_____

_____

Child's Name _____

Parent's Signature _____

Tareas escolares para la familia

Pronto vamos a comenzar con el nuevo tema de lectura llamado "¡Qué día!" Aprenderemos que cada día de nuestras vidas tiene algo especial. Para que su niño/a se familiarice con el tema, ayúdelo/la a identificar un día que para él/ella sea muy especial, e inolvidable.

Pídale que haga un dibujo de lo que sucedió ese día. Luego, ayúdelo/la a escribir un párrafo para describir ese día tan especial.

Un día inolvidable

_____

_____

_____

_____

_____

_____

_____

Nombre del/de la niño/a _____

Firma del padre, de la madre o del tutor _____

HOME PROJECT

Creating an Animated Cartoon

An animated cartoon is a drawing that seems to move. The secret is that it is not one drawing but many drawings, each slightly different from the one before it. Flipping the drawings as rapidly as possible makes the figures seem to move. With your help (or the help of another family member or friend), your child can create an animated cartoon. Have your child bring the completed project to school by _____ so that he or she can share the cartoon with the class.

STEP 1
Choosing a Topic

Help your child decide whom or what to show in motion. It could be a silly picture or a realistic one. It might be one of the following:

• a pig juggling an ice-cream cone
• an airplane landing
• a bear dancing
• a child running

Use your imagination, but keep the picture simple.

SHORTCUT

If you're short on time, you can speed up this project by having your child draw a stick figure or some other very simple sketch that has a minimum of details.

STEP 2
Drawing the Pictures

MATERIALS

- a small pad of paper (self-stick notes work well)
- pencil
- crayons or colored pencils

Every tiny movement in an animated cartoon is a separate picture. To keep the changes small from one picture to the next, have your child follow these steps:

1. Begin on the first page of a pad of paper. Using a pencil, draw the picture as it will look at the very beginning. Make the lines as dark as you can by pressing hard.
2. Go on to the next page. If you pressed hard enough, you will see the outline of your drawing. Trace the picture, but make one small change.
3. Do the same for each page that follows, being careful not to rip the pages from the pad.

STEP 3
Testing Your Flip Book

Have your child flip through the book quickly. The picture should seem to move. Try it a few times. Your child may need to redraw one or two pictures to make it work just right.

When your child is satisfied with the pictures, have him or her color them. Remember that it is the same scene in each picture—if a tree is dark green in one picture, it should be dark green in all the others (unless you're showing seasonal changes).

EXTENDING THE PROJECT
Your child might choose to extend the project in one or more of these ways:

- Write a story to go with the cartoon.
- Tape-record a "soundtrack" for the cartoon.
- Make another flip book.

TIP

If your child has trouble pressing hard enough, try working backwards. Have him or her begin on the last page of your pad and draw the action the way it will look when it ends. Then pull down the next page and *trace* the picture except for one small difference. Remind your child that he or she is working backwards.

PROYECTO PARA EL HOGAR

Cómo crear un dibujo animado

Un dibujo animado es un dibujo que da la impresión de tener movimiento. El secreto está en que no se trata de un dibujo, sino de varios. Cada uno de ellos es ligeramente distinto al anterior. Al pasarlos rápidamente, parece como que las figuras se mueven. Con su ayuda, o la de otro miembro de la familia o amigo, su niño/a puede crear un dibujo animado. Haga que su niño/a lleve el proyecto terminado a la escuela el _____ para que lo comparta con la clase.

PASO 1
Selección de un tema

Ayude a su niño/a a decidir qué cosa o a quién quiere mostrar en movimiento. Podría ser un dibujo gracioso o uno real. Por ejemplo:

- un cerdito haciendo malabarismos con el cono de un helado
- un avión en el momento de aterrizar
- un oso bailando
- un niño corriendo

Usen la imaginación, pero recuerden que el dibujo debe ser sencillo.

ALTERNATIVA

Si dispone de poco tiempo, puede acortar este proyecto haciendo que su niño/a haga un dibujo sencillo con pocos detalles.

PASO 2
Cómo hacer los dibujos

MATERIALES

- un bloc o anotador pequeño (como, por ejemploa, de esos que se pegan)
- lapicero
- creyones o lápices de colores

Todo movimiento de un dibujo animado es un dibujo distinto. Para que los cambios sean mínimos de un dibujo a otro, haga que su niño/a siga estos pasos:

1. En la primera página del bloc, haga el primer dibujo con lápiz. Marque las líneas con firmeza de modo que queden bien oscuras.
2. Pase a la página siguiente. Si se ha presionado el lápiz lo suficiente, se verá el contorno del dibujo. Trace el mismo dibujo, pero incorpore un pequeño cambio.
3. Haga lo mismo en las páginas siguientes, pero con cuidado para no arrancar las hojas del bloc.

PASO 3
Cómo probar el librito animado

Pasen las hojas del bloc rápidamente. La figura debe dar la idea de que se mueve. Háganlo unas cuantas veces. Es posible que haya que volver a dibujar una o más figuras para mejorar el efecto.

Cuando su niño/a esté satisfecho/a con los dibujos, pídale que los coloree. Recuerden que la escena debe mantenerse en todos los dibujos (si pintaron un árbol de color verde oscuro en un dibujo, tendrá que ser verde oscuro en el siguiente, a menos que quieran mostrar un cambio acelerado de estaciones).

AMPLIACIÓN DEL PROYECTO

Si su niño/a desea continuar con el proyecto, puede seguir alguna de estas propuestas:

- Escribir un relato que explique la acción.
- Grabar en una cinta de música la "banda musical" del dibujo animado.
- Hacer otro dibujo animado.

SUGERENCIA

Si su niño/a no puede presionar con firmeza el lápiz, haga que trabaje al revés. Puede comenzar en la última página y hacer el dibujo final. Luego, debe poner encima la página anterior y calcar la figura haciendo algo ligeramente diferente. Recuérdele que está trabajando de atrás hacia delante.

HOME PROJECT

Preparing a Neighborhood Guide

What are the important locations in your neighborhood? Where will a visitor find a place to play? A library? A mailbox? With your help (or the help of another family member or friend), your child can create a guide to your neighborhood. Have your child bring the completed project to school by _____ so that he or she can share the guide with the class.

STEP 1
Deciding on the Contents

With your child, decide what information the guidebook will contain. Guidebooks that are sold in stores tell readers about the following:

• scenic, historical, or unusual sights

• sporting events

• cultural activities

• shops and services

• places to eat

• getting help in an emergency

You may want to look through a few guidebooks together to help you plan your guide.

TIP

Remind your child to include the things that he or she likes best about your neighborhood!

SHORTCUT

If you're short on time, skip the rest of the project and simply plan to include places and topics with which your child is already familiar. Then help your child write a paragraph about each topic in a notebook. He or she can draw pictures to illustrate the guide.

STEP 2
Researching the Neighborhood

MATERIALS
- notebook
- paper
- pencils, pens
- stapler

optional:
- crayons or markers
- photographs
- glue or paste

Once you and your child have decided what the guidebook will contain, work together to complete these steps:

1. Write the name of each topic on a separate sheet of paper in a notebook.
2. Gather information about the topic and record it in the notebook.
3. Use the information to write a paragraph or two about each topic. Try to make it interesting to a stranger. What would a newcomer like to know about your neighborhood? What would he or she need to know?

STEP 3
Reviewing the Guidebook

Help your child check to be sure that the information in the guidebook is

- **Complete.** If the neighborhood swimming pool opens in June and closes on Labor Day, let your readers know.
- **Interesting.** Are any unusual or amazing facts about your neighborhood included? Where is the oldest building? Who has the most beautiful garden? The strangest pet?
- **Accurate.** You don't want anyone to get lost!
- **Clearly written.** Read your information aloud to each other to see if it makes sense.

Then organize your pages and number them. Work together to make a cover. Before you staple the book together, you might work with your child to add photographs or draw pictures of important places and events to illustrate your guide.

EXTENDING THE PROJECT
Your child might choose to extend the project in one or more of these ways:

- Write an advertisement for your neighborhood.
- Take a friend on a guided tour of the neighborhood.
- Write a paragraph about a favorite place in the neighborhood.

PROYECTO PARA EL HOGAR

Preparación de una guía del vecindario

¿Cuáles son los sitios importantes de su vecindario? ¿En qué lugar podría jugar un visitante? ¿Dónde hallaría una biblioteca? ¿Un buzón? Con su ayuda, o la de otro miembro de la familia o amigo, su niño/a puede hacer una guía del vecindario. Haga que su niño/a lleve el proyecto terminado a la escuela el _____ para compartirlo con la clase.

PASO 1
Decisión acerca del contenido de la guía

Pónganse de acuerdo usted y su niño/a para decidir el contenido de la guía. Las guías que se venden en las tiendas informan al lector sobre lo siguiente:

• vistas panorámicas, sitios históricos o especiales

• eventos deportivos

• actividades culturales

• tiendas y otros servicios

• restaurantes

• a quién se debe acudir en caso de emergencias

Podrían hojear juntos algunas guías para tomar ideas

SUGERENCIA

¡Recuérdele a su niño/a que incluya las cosas que más le gustan del vecindario!

ALTERNATIVA

Si dispone de poco tiempo, en lugar de hacer el resto del proyecto, considere los lugares y temas conocidos por su niño/a. Luego, ayúdelo/la a escribir en el cuaderno un párrafo sobre cada uno. Finalmente, su niño/a puede hacer dibujos para ilustrar la guía.

PASO 2
Investigación sobre el vecindario

MATERIALES

- cuaderno
- papel
- lápices, bolígrafos
- grapadora

opcional:

- creyones o marcadores
- fotos
- pegamento o cola

Una vez que hayan decidido el contenido de la guía, completen los siguientes pasos:

1. Escriban el nombre de cada tema en una hoja distinta del cuaderno.
2. Reúnan datos acerca del tema, y escríbanlos en el cuaderno.
3. Usen estos datos para escribir un párrafo o dos acerca de cada tema. Traten de que sea interesante para una persona que no conozca el vecindario. ¿Qué le gustaría saber del vecindario a un visitante? ¿Qué necesitaría saber?

PASO 3
Revisión de la guía

Ayude a su niño/a a comprobar que la información de la guía sea:

- **Completa:** Si la piscina del vecindario abre en junio y cierra el Día del Trabajo, háganselo saber a los lectores.
- **Interesante:** ¿Incluyeron datos raros o sorprendentes acerca del vecindario? ¿Dónde está el edificio más antiguo? ¿Quién tiene el jardín más hermoso? ¿Y la mascota más extraña?
- **Precisa:** ¡No quieren que nadie se pierda!
- **Escrita de forma clara:** Vuelvan a leer la guía entre ustedes para comprobar que la información tiene sentido.

Luego, organicen las páginas y enumérenlas. Hagan una cubierta para la guía. Antes de engrapar las hojas, su niño/a podría agregar fotos o hacer dibujos de los sucesos y lugares importantes para ilustrar la guía.

AMPLIACIÓN DEL PROYECTO
Si su niño/a desea continuar con el proyecto, puede seguir alguna de estas propuestas:

- Escribir un anuncio para el vecindario.
- Llevar a un amigo a dar un paseo por el vecindario, siendo su niño/a el/la guía.
- Escribir un párrafo sobre un lugar favorito en el vecindario.

HOME PROJECT

Conducting a Fire Safety Survey

Most fires can be prevented. With your help (or the help of another family member or friend), your child can check your home for fire hazards. Have your child bring the completed project to school by _____ so that he or she can share the survey with the class.

STEP 1
Gathering Information

With your child, visit the library or contact your local fire station for information about fire safety. The information you gather should answer the following questions:

- What is the cause of most household fires?
- Where are household fires most likely to start?
- What can be done to keep a fire from starting?
- What can be done in case of a fire?

TIP

Exchange ideas about how a fire could start in each room, including the basement, the attic, and/or the garage.

SHORTCUT

If you're short on time, instead of the survey, work together to plan escape routes from your home in case of fire. Draw a map showing where to exit and where to meet outside. After sharing the map at school, you can post it in a central location in your home.

STEP 2
Designing a Checklist

MATERIALS

- a sheet of paper for each room in your home
- pencil or pen

optional:

- clipboard

Help your child use the information to make a checklist for every room in your home. A checklist for the kitchen might include the following questions:

- How many extension cords are in use?
- How many appliances are plugged into each outlet?
- Are cleaning supplies stored near the stove?
- Are matches within reach of young children?
- Is there a smoke detector in the kitchen or nearby?

What questions might be asked about the other rooms in your home? After you have completed your checklist for all rooms, use it to determine how safe your house or apartment is.

STEP 3
Sharing the Results

As a family, discuss the results of your survey. Plan ways to make your house or apartment a safer place to live. Then set aside a day to carry out your plan.

EXTENDING THE PROJECT

Your child might choose to extend the project in one or more of these ways:

- Repeat the survey in two months. Is your home safer than it was when you completed the first survey?
- Draw a map showing every exit from your house and which would be best to use in case of a fire. The map should also show a family meeting place outside your home.
- Create a poster or booklet that teaches kindergartners about fire safety.

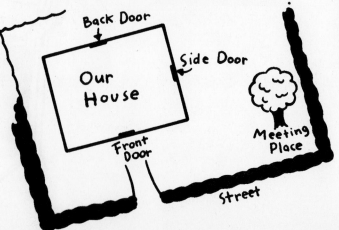

PROYECTO PARA EL HOGAR

Cómo inspeccionar la casa para prevenir incendios

Es posible prevenir la mayoría de los incendios. Con su ayuda, o la de otro miembro de la familia o amigo, su niño/a puede revisar la casa en busca de situaciones que suelen provocar incendios. Haga que su niño/a lleve el proyecto terminado a la escuela el _____ para que lo comparta con la clase.

PASO 1
Recopilación de información

Visiten la biblioteca o llamen a la estación de bomberos para conseguir información acerca de cómo prevenir incendios. La información que obtengan deberá responder a las siguientes preguntas:

- ¿Cuál es la causa de la mayoría de los incendios en el hogar?

- ¿En qué habitaciones de la casa se originan la mayoría de los incendios?

- ¿Qué se debe hacer para prevenir un incendio?

- ¿Qué se debe hacer en caso de incendio?

SUGERENCIA

Intercambien ideas sobre la manera en que podría producirse un incendio en cada habitación, incluido el sótano, el ático y/o el garaje.

ALTERNATIVA

Si dispone de poco tiempo, en lugar de hacer éstas averiguaciones, hagan un plan de escape en caso de incendio. Hagan un plano de la casa; señalen las rutas de salida y un sitio de reunión afuera de la casa. Después de compartirlo con la clase, pueden ponerlo en un lugar bien visible de su hogar.

PASO 2
Cómo diseñar una lista

MATERIALES

- una hoja de papel para cada habitación de su casa
- lapicero o bolígrafo

opcional:

- tablilla con sujetapapeles

Ayude a su niño/a a usar la información para hacer una lista de prevención de incendios para cada habitación. Una lista para la cocina, tendría las siguientes preguntas.

- ¿Cuántos cables prolongadores se están usando?
- ¿Cuántos aparatos están enchufados en cada toma eléctrica?
- ¿Están los productos de limpieza cerca de la estufa o del horno?
- ¿Hay fósforos al alcance de los niños pequeños?
- ¿Hay un detector de humo en la cocina o cerca de ella?

¿Qué preguntas podrían aplicarse a otras habitaciones en su casa?

Cuando la lista esté completa, averigüen lo segura que es la casa o el apartamento donde viven.

PASO 3
Cómo compartir los resultados

Reúnanse en familia para hablar de los resultados de la inspección. Propongan un plan para mejorar la seguridad de la vivienda. Luego, escojan un día para llevar a cabo el plan.

AMPLIACIÓN DEL PROYECTO

Si su niño/a desea continuar con el proyecto, puede seguir alguna de estas propuestas:

- Repetir la inspección a los dos meses. ¿Es más segura la casa que cuando hicieron la primera inspección?
- Hacer un plano de la casa que muestre todas las salidas, y señalar la más apropiada en caso de incendio. Podrán también indicar un sitio de reunión fuera de la casa.
- Hacer un cartel o folleto con reglas de seguridad en caso de incendio, para enseñar a los niños del jardín de infantes.

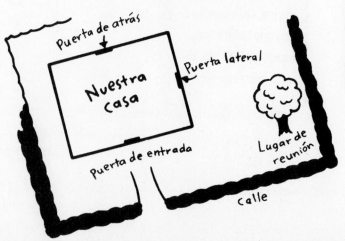

HOME PROJECT

Conducting a Taste Test

Why do some foods taste good while others don't? With your help (or the help of another family member or friend), your child can explore answers to this question. Have your child bring the completed project to school by _____ so that he or she can share the results with the class.

STEP 1
Making Predictions

Interview each other about the kind of foods you like and don't like. Then discuss these questions:

- How do the taste buds on your tongue work? Does where you put food on your tongue affect the way the food tastes?

- How does the smell of food contribute to the way it tastes? Would an apple taste as good if it smelled like an onion?

- What about the way food looks? Would a slice of bread taste any different if it were purple?

Invite your child to make predictions about answers to these questions before beginning the experiments in Step 2. Discuss the reasons for each prediction.

TIP

While completing the rest of the experiment, do what scientists do—keep track of exactly how each part of the experiment is carried out. Exactly where on your tongue did you taste the sugar cube? How much food coloring did you put in the milk?

SHORTCUT

If you're short on time, pick just one experiment to do, and then move on to Step 3.

STEP 2
Experimenting with Taste

MATERIALS

- sugar cubes
- salt
- lemon juice
- onion
- apple
- piece of candy
- milk or juice
- food coloring
- paper
- pencil

With your child, try the following experiments.

Where's the taste on your tongue? Place a sugar cube on different parts of your tongue. Where do you actually taste it? Try the same experiment with salt and then lemon juice. You may want to try other foods too. Do you taste each on the same part of your tongue?

What does the nose know? Hold a peeled onion to your nose. While you smell it, bite into an apple. How does the apple taste? Place a piece of candy in your mouth while you smell the onion.

Do looks count? Place a little red or blue food coloring in some milk or juice. Then taste it. Does it taste different than normal?

STEP 3
Recording the Results

What did the taste tests show? Have your child write a paragraph describing the results of each experiment the two of you did. Remind your child to include his or her earlier predictions, and how they compared to the results.

EXTENDING THE PROJECT

Your child might choose to extend the project in one or more of these ways:

- Try each experiment on family members and friends and record the results. Did they respond the way you did? How do you explain any differences?
- Try the experiments with different foods to see if the results change.
- Map your tongue! Where on your tongue do you taste sweet things? Salty things? Sour foods? Bitter ones?

PROYECTO PARA EL HOGAR

Experimentos con sabores

¿Por qué algunas comidas tienen buen sabor y otras no? Con su ayuda, o la de otro miembro de la familia o amigo, su niño/a puede averiguar la respuesta a esta pregunta. Haga que su niño/a lleve el proyecto terminado a la escuela el _____ para que lo comparta con la clase.

PASO 1
Cómo hacer predicciones

Entrevístense el uno al otro para averiguar el tipo de comidas que le gusta a cada uno. Luego, traten de responder a estas preguntas:

- ¿Qué función cumplen las papilas gustativas de la lengua? El lugar de la lengua donde se pone la comida, ¿tiene algún efecto en su sabor?

- ¿El olor de la comida tiene alguna influencia en su sabor? ¿Seguiría siendo sabrosa una manzana si tuviera olor a cebolla?

- ¿Qué piensan del aspecto de la comida? ¿Cambiaría el sabor del pan si fuera de color morado?

Pídale a su niño/a que prediga las respuestas antes de hacer los experimentos del paso 2 que vienen a continuación. Pídale que le explique en qué se basan sus predicciones y hablen sobre ello.

SUGERENCIA

Mientras completan el resto del experimento, hagan como los científicos; tomen notas detalladas de todos los pasos del experimento. Expliquen exactamente con qué parte de la lengua sintieron el sabor del cubito de azúcar. ¿Qué cantidad de colorante para comida pusieron en la leche?

ALTERNATIVA

Si dispone de poco tiempo, hagan un solo experimento y luego completen el paso 3.

PASO 2
Experimentos con el gusto

MATERIALES

- cubitos de azúcar
- sal
- jugo de limón
- cebolla
- manzana
- un caramelo u otro dulce
- leche o jugo
- colorantes para comida
- papel
- lapicero

Hagan usted y su niño/a los siguientes experimentos:

¿En qué parte de la lengua está el gusto?
Pónganse un cubito de azúcar en distintas partes de la lengua. ¿En dónde pueden notar el sabor? Hagan el mismo experimento con sal y luego con jugo de limón. Si lo desean, también pueden hacer la prueba con otras comidas. ¿Sienten el sabor de todas las comidas con la misma parte de la lengua?

¿Qué sabe la nariz? Pónganse una cebolla pelada cerca de la nariz. Mientras la huelen, muerdan una manzana. ¿Qué gusto tiene la manzana? Pónganse un caramelo en la boca mientras huelen la cebolla. ¿Qué gusto tiene el caramelo?

¿Es importante la apariencia?
Agréguenle a la leche o al jugo unas gotas de colorante para comida que sean de color rojo o azul. Luego, tomen un poquito de este líquido. ¿Ha cambiado el sabor?

PASO 3
Anotación de los resultados

¿Qué comprobaron con los experimentos? Haga que su niño/a escriba un párrafo para describir los resultados de cada experimento que hayan realizado. Recuérdele a su niño/a que incluya sus predicciones previas, y que las compare con los resultados.

AMPLIACIÓN DEL PROYECTO
Si su niño/a desea continuar con el proyecto, puede seguir alguna de estas propuestas:

- Realizar los experimentos con familiares y amigos y anotar los resultados. ¿Hay diferencias con lo que ustedes comprobaron? ¿Cómo pueden explicarlas?
- Cambiar los alimentos a la hora de hacer los experimentos para observar si varían los resultados.
- ¡Trazar un mapa de la lengua! ¿En qué parte de la lengua degustan los dulces? ¿Y las comidas saladas, o las agrias? ¿Y las amargas?

HOME PROJECT

Charting the Weather

What can you learn by observing the weather in your community? With your help (or the help of another family member or friend), your child can keep track of the weather in your community for several weeks. Have your child bring the completed project to school by _____ so that he or she can share the weather chart with the class.

STEP 1
Recording the Weather

Discuss what information to collect about the weather. Here are several possibilities:

- temperature (morning, afternoon, evening)
- rainfall or snowfall (inches per day)
- number of sunny, cloudy, and rainy days
- wind (light breeze, occasional gusts, strong winds)
- hottest/coldest days

Brainstorm where to find the information you track. How much information can be gathered from observation? From newspaper, radio, or TV?

BAR GRAPH

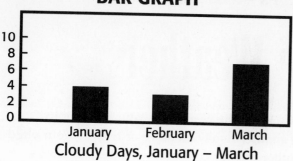

Cloudy Days, January – March

PICTOGRAPH

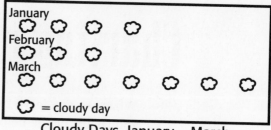

Cloudy Days, January – March

STEP 2
Recording Information

MATERIALS

- a spiral notebook or a calendar
- graph paper
- pencil or pen
- crayons

Your child may choose to record information about the weather on a calendar. Or, he or she might prefer to keep a weather diary in a spiral notebook. Either way, track the weather for at least two weeks. Set aside a few minutes at the end of each day to discuss the weather and write down the day's statistics.

SHORTCUT

If you're short on time, stop here and have your child take the calendar or notebook to school.

STEP 3
Graphing the Results

Graphs are a special way to show information. The drawings on this page show two ways you can graph information. One is a bar graph, and the other is a pictograph. Depending on what facts are collected, you might help your child graph the following:

- sunny, cloudy, and rainy days
- high and low daily temperatures
- rainfall and/or snowfall
- hottest/coldest days

EXTENDING THE PROJECT
Your child might choose to extend the project in one or more of these ways:

- Write a paragraph describing a trend in the weather. During the time you collected information, was the weather getting warmer? Wetter? Windier?
- Keep track of the weather in a similar fashion at another season of the year. Then compare findings.
- Using information from the newspaper or TV, keep track of the weather for a city in another part of the country or the world. How is the weather there like the weather in your community? How is it different?

PROYECTO PARA EL HOGAR

Cómo hacer una gráfica del tiempo atmosférico

¿Qué podemos aprender al observar el tiempo del lugar donde vivimos? Con su ayuda, o la de otro miembro de la familia o amigo, su niño/a puede llevar un registro del tiempo atmosférico durante varias semanas. Haga que su niño/a lleve el proyecto terminado a la escuela el _____ para que lo comparta con la clase.

PASO 1
Cómo llevar un registro del tiempo atmosférico

Decidan el tipo de información que desean averiguar acerca del tiempo. Éstas son algunas de las posibilidades:

- temperatura (mañana, tarde, noche)
- cantidad de lluvia o nieve (pulgadas por día)
- número de días soleados, nublados o lluviosos
- viento (brisa, ráfagas de viento, vientos fuertes)
- días más calurosos y más fríos

Piensen en dónde podrán hallar los datos que buscan. ¿Cuántos datos se pueden averiguar con la simple observación? ¿Y en los periódicos, la radio o la televisión?

GRÁFICA DE BARRAS

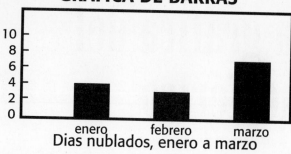

Dias nublados, enero a marzo

PICTOGRAMA

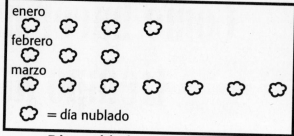

Días nublados, enero a marzo

PASO 2
Anotación de los datos

MATERIALES

- un cuaderno de espiral o un calendario
- papel cuadriculado
- lapicero o bolígrafo
- creyones

Su niño/a podría decidir anotar los datos del tiempo atmosférico en un calendario, o bien mantener un diario del mismo en un cuaderno de espiral. Haga lo que haga, debe registrar los datos del tiempo como mínimo durante dos semanas. Reserven unos minutos al final de cada día para que su niño/a escriba la información de la jornada.

ALTERNATIVA

Si dispone de poco tiempo, terminen aquí el proyecto y asegúrese de que su niño/a lo lleve a la escuela.

PASO 3
Cómo representar los resultados en una gráfica

Las gráficas permiten mostrar información de una manera especial. En esta página pueden observar dos tipos de gráficas: una gráfica de barras y un pictograma. Según los datos reunidos, podrá ayudar a su niño/a a hacer una gráfica de lo siguiente:

- días soleados, nublados y lluviosos
- temperatura mínima y máxima de cada día
- cantidad de lluvia y/o nieve
- días más calurosos y más fríos

AMPLIACIÓN DEL PROYECTO

Si su niño/a desea continuar con el proyecto, puede seguir alguna de estas propuestas:

- Escribir un párrafo sobre una tendencia del tiempo. Durante el período observado, ¿aumentó la temperatura? ¿Y la humedad o el viento?
- Anotar los datos del tiempo en otra estación del año. Luego, se podrán comparar los dos registros del tiempo.
- Utilizar la información de los periódicos o de la televisión, para llevar un registro del tiempo en una ciudad de otra parte del país o del mundo. Se podrán observar los parecidos y las diferencias entre el clima de esa ciudad y el lugar donde viven.

HOME PROJECT

Making a Poster for a Special Day

Was it an ordinary day or an extraordinary one? With your help (or the help of another family member or friend), your child can explore the events in a single day and then create a poster celebrating the day. Have your child bring the completed project to school by _____ so that he or she can share the poster with the class.

STEP 1
Researching the Day

MATERIALS
- note paper
- pencil or pen
- poster board or shelving paper or a large paper bag cut open to lie flat
- crayons or markers

optional:
- pictures cut from old magazines, calendars, or newspapers
- paste or glue
- newspaper, almanac, calendar

TIP

Be sure to record what you learn from your reading and interviews.

With your child, choose a day to research. It might be today. Or your child may want to choose a special day like his or her birthday or a holiday. Have your child do the following:

- List the things that happened to him or her that day.
- Interview family members, friends, and neighbors about what happened to them.
- Watch the evening news or read a newspaper for events of the day (if your child chose today).
- Look through almanacs and calendars to find out what happened on that day in history. (Many newspapers carry a feature called "On This Day in History." It can be a good source of information.)
- Check weather reports. What was the weather like? Were any records broken that day?

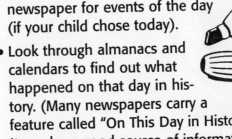

SHORTCUT

If you're short on time, pick today, your child's birthday, or a favorite holiday. Then, rather than doing research, complete the rest of the project based on your child's personal experience.

STEP 2
Sorting the Information

After your child has gathered all the information, help him or her organize the notes. You might sort them according to

- where they occurred—school, home, community, state, nation, world
- when they happened—long ago, last year, today

Next, decide what it is about the day that the two of you want to celebrate on the poster. You might focus on why this was an important day in history—or just an important day for you and your child.

STEP 3
Making the Poster

Help your child create a poster about the day. You can do the following:

- Create your own art.
- Glue on pictures from magazines, headlines from newspapers, or mementos of the day.
- Record quotes from TV or radio reports or from famous people.

Give the poster a title that indicates why this day is so special.

EXTENDING THE PROJECT

Your child might choose to extend the project in one or more of these ways:

- Write a story based on one event shown on the poster.
- Create a similar poster for a day that occurs at a different season of the year.
- Write a paragraph or two about who would celebrate this day and how they would celebrate it.

PROYECTO PARA EL HOGAR

Cómo hacer un cartel sobre un día especial

¿Fue un día como todos o un día extraordinario? Con su ayuda, o la de otro miembro de la familia o amigo, su niño/a puede explorar los sucesos ocurridos en un día y crear un cartel para celebrar esa jornada. Haga que su niño/a lleve el proyecto terminado a la escuela el _____ para compartirlo con la clase.

PASO 1
Cómo investigar el día

MATERIALES

- papel para tomar notas
- lapicero o bolígrafo
- cartulina o papel para estanterías o una bolsa grande de papel cortada a lo largo y abierta
- creyones o marcadores

opcional:

- ilustraciones de revistas, calendarios o periódicos viejos
- pegamento o cola
- periódico, almanaque, calendario

SUGERENCIA

Asegúrense de anotar lo que averiguaron con las lecturas y entrevistas.

Escojan usted y su hijo/a el día que deseen investigar. Podría ser hoy; o quizá su niño/a desee escoger una fecha especial, como el día de su cumpleaños o un día de fiesta. Pídale que haga lo siguiente:

- Hacer una lista con las actividades que realizó él/ella ese día.

- Entrevistar a los familiares, amigos y vecinos para averiguar lo que hicieron ellos.

- Mirar el noticiero de la tarde o busque en el periódico las actividades que están previstas para hoy (si el día escogido fue hoy).

- Averiguar en almanaques o calendarios lo que pasó ese mismo día en años anteriores. (Muchos periódicos suelen tener una sección llamada "Hoy en la historia", u otro nombre similar, que es una buena fuente de información.)

- Leer los reportes del tiempo. ¿Qué tiempo hizo? ¿Se superó algún récord ese día?

ALTERNATIVA

Si dispone de poco tiempo, pídale a su niño/a que escoja hoy, su día de cumpleaños o su día feriado preferido. Luego, en lugar de hacer la investigación, completen el proyecto basándose en la experiencia personal de su niño/a.

PASO 2
Cómo ordenar la información

Después de que su niño/a haya reunido todos los datos, ayúdelo/la a ordenar las notas. Podrían organizarlas según lo siguiente:

• el sitio donde ocurrieron los hechos: la escuela, la casa, el vecindario, el estado, el país, el mundo

• la fecha en que ocurrieron: hace mucho tiempo, el año pasado, hoy

Luego, escojan entre ambos los acontecimientos que quieran celebrar en el cartel. Podrían centrarse en la importancia histórica de esa fecha, o bien referirse a lo que ese día representa para usted y su niño/a.

PASO 3
Cómo hacer el cartel

Hagan usted y su niño/a un cartel referido al día que escogieron. Su niño/a podría hacer lo siguiente:

• Crear sus propias ilustraciones.

• Pegar recortes de revistas, titulares de periódicos o recuerdos del día

• Anotar citas de periodistas de radio o televisión o de gente famosa.

Pónganle un título que resalte la importancia del día.

AMPLIACIÓN DEL PROYECTO

Si su niño/a desea continuar con el proyecto, puede seguir alguna de estas propuestas:

• Escribir un relato basándose en un suceso registrado en el cartel.

• Crear un cartel similar para un día de otra estación del año.

• Escribir un párrafo o dos acerca de las personas que celebrarían ese día, y cómo lo harían.

HOME PROJECT

Evaluation

Please help me improve the home project experience in the future by answering the following questions. Your child can return the form to school with the completed project. Thanks so much for your help.

Name of Home Project: _____

Name of person who helped child with the project: _____

Please circle the relationship of that person to the child.

Mother   Father   Brother   Sister   Grandparent   Friend   Other _____

How would you rate this project?

❏ Terrific   ❏ Good   ❏ Okay   ❏ Difficult   ❏ Not very interesting

How does your child rate this project?

❏ Terrific   ❏ Good   ❏ Okay   ❏ Difficult   ❏ Not very interesting

Do you think the project provided a worthwhile activity for your child? Why or why not?

_____

_____

_____

_____

What changes would improve the project?

_____

_____

_____

_____

Please add any additional comments that you want to make.

_____

_____

_____

_____

Evaluación de los proyectos para el hogar

La información requerida en este formulario me permitirá mejorar la experiencia de los proyectos para el hogar. Por favor, complételo y envíelo con su niño/a a la escuela junto con el proyecto terminado. Muchas gracias por su colaboración.

Nombre del proyecto: _____

Persona que ayudó al estudiante a hacer el proyecto: _____

Por favor, haga un círculo alrededor de la relación de esa persona con el estudiante.

Madre   Padre   Hermano   Hermana   Abuelo/a   Amigo/a   Otro _____

¿Cómo calificaría usted este proyecto?

❑ Excelente   ❑ Bueno   ❑ Aceptable   ❑ Difícil   ❑ Poco interesante

¿Cómo calificaría su niño/a al proyecto?

❑ Excelente   ❑ Bueno   ❑ Aceptable   ❑ Difícil   ❑ Poco interesante

¿Considera que este proyecto fue una actividad productiva para su niño/a? ¿Por qué?

_____

_____

_____

¿Qué cambios haría para mejorar el proyecto?

_____

_____

_____

Se desea hacer algún comentario, utilice por favor el espacio siguiente.

_____

_____

_____

Parent–Teacher–Child Dialogue

The form below is one that we can use to have a parent-teacher-child dialogue. Anyone can start the dialogue, at any time, about anything. Let's try to answer one another as promptly as possible. We should also let one another know at any time if we'd prefer to talk or meet in person instead of using the form. I will send another blank form home each time we complete one.

Parent's Comments

Dear _____

Date _____

Sincerely,

_____

Teacher's Comments

Dear _____

Date _____

Sincerely,

_____

Child's Comments

Dear _____

Date _____

Sincerely,

_____

Diálogo entre maestro, estudiante y familiar

Para la comunicación entre maestro, familia y estudiante, usaremos el formulario de abajo. Cualquiera puede iniciar el diálogo, en cualquier momento y sobre cualquier tema. Por favor, escriba todo comentario que desee hacer de la manera que sea más conveniente para usted. Puede escribirlos en inglés —o pedirle a alguien que se los escriba— o en español (y yo los haré traducir). Tratemos de responder lo más pronto posible y de avisarnos si queremos conversar personalmente, en lugar de usar el formulario. Enviaré un formulario en blanco a la casa cada vez que hayamos completado el anterior.

Comentarios de los familiares

Estimado/a _____   Fecha _____

Atentamente, _____

Comentarios del estudiante

Estimado/a _____

Comentarios del maestro

Estimado/a _____   Fecha _____

Atentamente, _____

Atentamente, _____

Help Your Child Become a Successful Reader

Do you know how children become good readers? They read. The more a child reads, the better reader he or she will become. Of all the things you can do to help your child at school, the most *important* thing you can do is to make sure your child spends time at home reading. This short article will tell you why it is important that you encourage your child to read, and give you some ideas for doing so.

What We Know

- Almost every time your child reads a book, he or she learns something about people, or a place, or a topic, or an idea. What is learned becomes your child's background information. The more background information a reader has, the easier it is for him or her to understand new information in other books.

- Reading increases the vocabulary. The more your child reads, the more words he or she learns. Children who read widely can learn the meanings of thousands of new words each year.

How You Can Help

- **Make books available at home.**
  Plan trips to the library or the bookstore. Give books for special occasions.

- **Find out your child's interests.**
  Help him or her find books to support this interest. Children *will* read if they have books that interest them and are appropriate for their reading level.

- **Set aside quiet time for reading.**
  Set aside 10–15 minutes each day for reading—after dinner, before bedtime, or at some other time during the day. Of course, there will be some days when this just isn't possible. That's all right, but you might try to spend a little extra time the next day.

- **Read aloud to your child.**
  Being read to is a treat that all children—and even adults—can enjoy. Take turns. Sometimes you can read to your child, and sometimes he or she can read to you. It's a great way to share time and interests.

- **Be a reading model.**
  Let your child see you reading for pleasure. Seeing how much you enjoy reading will help your child see that reading can be fun to do.

Cómo ayudar a que su niño/a adquiera el hábito de la lectura

¿Qué hacen los niños para aprender a leer bien? Leen. Cuanto más lea un niño, mejor lector será. De todas las cosas que usted puede hacer para ayudar a su niño/a a ser un buen estudiante, *la más importante* es asegurarse de que lea en casa. Este breve artículo le explicará por qué es importante que usted aliente el hábito de la lectura en su niño/a y le proporcionará algunas ideas sobre cómo hacerlo.

Lo que sabemos

- Cada vez que el niño o la niña lea un libro, aprenderá algo sobre gente, lugares, temas o ideas, y enriquecerá sus conocimientos generales. Cuantos más conocimientos generales tiene un lector, más fácil le resulta entender la información de nuevos libros.

- La lectura enriquece el vocabulario. Cuanto más lea su niño/a, más palabras aprenderá. Los niños que leen mucho pueden aprender el significado de miles de palabras por año.

Qué puede hacer usted

- **Asegurarse de que haya libros en la casa.**
  Planifiquen visitas a bibliotecas o librerías. Regálele libros en ocasiones especiales.

- **Averiguar los temas que le interesan a su niño/a.**
  Ayude a su niño/a a conseguir libros sobre cuestiones que le interesen. Los niños *sí* leen cuando disponen de libros que despiertan su interés y que son adecuados para su nivel de lectura.

- **Disponer de momentos libres para leer.**
  Es importante dedicar a la lectura unos 10 o 15 minutos por día —después de comer, antes de acostarse o a cualquier otra hora. Habrá días que será imposible hacerlo, pero al día siguiente hay que tratar de leer un poquito más.

- **Leer en voz alta para su niño/a.**
  Niños y grandes disfrutan cuando alguien les lee. Túrnense con su niño/a para leer en voz alta. Ésta es una excelente manera de pasar el tiempo y de compartir intereses.

- **Sea un lector modelo.**
  Deje que su niño/a vea que usted disfruta de la lectura. Su ejemplo le enseñará lo entretenido que es leer.

The Writing Process

Stories, poems, reports, articles—students do a lot of writing in school. Studies have shown that a good way to teach writing is through a series of steps modeled on the process that "real" writers use to develop their ideas.

Professional writers don't expect to express their ideas perfectly the first time they write them. Instead, they go through a process of rereading and revising to improve their writing.

Stages of the Writing Process

- prewriting—thinking of ideas to write about
- drafting—putting ideas down on paper without worrying about mistakes in spelling, grammar, or punctuation
- revising—reading the draft; having a conference with classmates or the teacher to get ideas on how the writing could be improved; making changes so that all the ideas in the writing make sense
- proofreading—correcting grammar, punctuation, and spelling
- publishing—sharing the finished piece in some way with others

In an effort to get all their ideas written down, students often write first drafts that include mistakes in grammar, spelling, punctuation, and organization. As they revise and proofread, they will be refining their work. They will notice some errors and correct them by themselves. In conferences the teacher and their classmates will point out errors the writers have not noticed.

How You Can Help

Check with your child's teacher.
Ask what you can do to help your child's writing efforts.

Help your child think of ideas to write about.
Talk together about your child's interests, friends, goals, hobbies, or favorite things (books, movies, clothes, television programs).

During the revising stage, read or listen to your child's writing.
Focus on the ideas. Point out something you really like. Ask questions about anything that isn't clear. This helps your child see what to change to make the writing clearer.

Don't be critical.
Let your child experiment with the process of writing and expressing ideas. Your child's teacher will guide spelling, grammar, and punctuation changes. Look for improvement from month to month, not perfection. Comment on the positive aspects, not the negative.

Read or listen to your child's finished writing.
Comment on your child's writing. Praise improvements. Let your child know that you think his or her writing is important. If your child would like to share his or her writing at home, try putting it on the refrigerator or in another common area. So that you and your child are able to see the progress that he or she makes over time, you might want to keep a scrapbook of your child's writing.

El proceso de escritura

En la escuela, los estudiantes redactan cuentos, poemas, informes y artículos. Los estudios realizados demuestran que un buen método para enseñar a escribir consiste en seguir una serie de pasos, como el proceso que usan los escritores profesionales para desarrollar sus ideas.

En lugar de tratar de expresar perfectamente sus ideas la primera vez que las escriben, los escritores profesionales releen y revisan lo que han escrito para mejorarlo.

Etapas del proceso de escritura

- pre-escritura: búsqueda de ideas
- borrador: poner las ideas en el papel sin preocuparse por los errores de ortografía, gramática o puntuación
- revisión: leer el borrador; hablar con los compañeros, o con la maestra o el maestro, para ver cómo se puede mejorar la redacción; hacer cambios para darle sentido a la composición
- corrección: corregir la gramática, puntuación y ortografía
- publicación: hacer pública la redacción para que otros la lean

En sus borradores, los estudiantes suelen concentrarse en escribir todas las ideas y cometen errores de gramática, ortografía, puntuación y organización. A medida que revisan su trabajo, van encontrando algunos errores y corrigiéndolos. Las entrevistas con los compañeros de clase y los maestros les sirven para hallar los errores que ellos no habían logrado detectar.

Cómo puede ayudar

Consulte con la maestra o el maestro.
Pregúntele cómo puede ayudar a su niño/a a aprender a escribir.

Ayude a su niño/a a buscar ideas o temas de redacción.
Platiquen sobre los intereses, amigos, deseos, pasatiempos o cosas favoritas (libros, películas, ropa, programas de televisión) de su niño/a.

Durante la etapa de revisión, lea o haga que su niño/a le lea lo que ha escrito.
Céntrese en las ideas. Señale algo que le guste. Haga preguntas sobre los puntos que no estén claros. Sus comentarios contribuirán a que su niño/a haga cambios para clarificar su redacción.

No tenga una actitud crítica.
Deje que su niño/a experimente con el proceso de escribir y expresar ideas. La maestra o el maestro lo/la ayudarán a corregir la ortografía, gramática y puntuación. No espere perfección, sino mejoras progresivas. En sus comentarios, céntrese en los aspectos positivos.

Lea su trabajo terminado o pídale a su niño/a que se lo lea.
Haga comentarios sobre la redacción; elogie las mejoras. Asegúrese de que su niño/a sepa que usted valora sus trabajos escritos. Si su niño/a desea exhibir su redacción en la casa, pueden colocarla en la puerta del refrigerador o en otro sitio similar. Para observar sus progresos, podrían hacer un álbum de recortes con los trabajos de redacción.

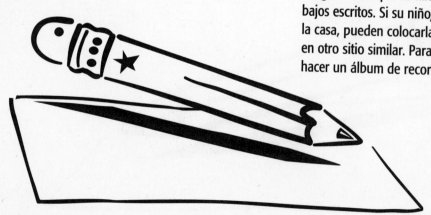

Handling Homework

"I have *tons* of homework. How will I ever get it all done?"

"Where's your homework?"
"I don't have any."
"Are you sure? You haven't had any all week."

"It's time for bed. See you in the morning."
"Oh no, I forgot! I have homework!"

You've probably heard or been a part of at least one of these conversations. Here are some things you can do to eliminate the problems of homework at your house:

Make and follow a homework schedule.
Limit TV time. With your child, decide on a specific time each day to do schoolwork. If the time varies due to other activities, prepare a daily schedule. Planning a homework schedule will help your child organize his or her time—and cut down on the amount of monitoring you have to do.

Find out what to expect.
Ask your child's teacher about his or her homework policies so that you will know if and when to expect homework assignments. If your child is not given a homework assignment, the scheduled time can be used for reading for pleasure.

Provide a place for your child to study.
Try to provide a quiet, well-lighted place for your child to study. Make sure there is room for books, paper, pencils, and whatever else is needed. Turn off noisy distractions such as a TV or stereo in the study area. Encourage other family members to respect the quiet place where schoolwork is being done.

Help your child understand assignments.
Ask your child to keep an assignment list or notebook. For each task, clarify the directions. If necessary, give an example to show how to do the work. Then discuss with your child how he or she plans to go about completing the assignment.

Don't do the homework for your child.
Completing the assignment independently will help your child learn. Your child will also feel a sense of pride in doing the work on his or her own. If your child is unable to complete the work independently, talk with the teacher about how to help your child.

Provide support.
Support can take many forms:

- Offer to quiz your child on material for a test.
- When a library visit is necessary to complete an assignment or project, make sure your child is able to get there.
- Show interest in your child's homework. Ask if he or she wants you to check the assignment.
- Praise your child as he or she grows in accepting responsibility for homework.

Setting the stage for good homework habits will be beneficial not only now, but also later when your child moves into higher grades where the amount of homework often increases.

Las tareas escolares

—Tengo *muchísimas* tareas. ¿Cómo podré hacerlo todo?

—¿Tienes tareas para mañana?
—No tengo nada que hacer.
—¿Estás segura? No has tenido ninguna tarea en toda la semana.

—Es hora de ir a la cama. Hasta mañana.
—¡Oh, no! ¡Me olvidé de que tenía que hacer mis tareas!

Es muy probable que usted haya escuchado alguna de estas conversaciones. Para reducir los problemas con las tareas escolares le proponemos las siguientes ideas:

Preparen un horario para realizar las tareas.
Limite el tiempo dedicado a mirar televisión. De acuerdo con su niño/a, establezcan un momento determinado del día para hacer el trabajo de la escuela. Preparen un horario para cada día si hay variaciones debidas a otras actividades. La planificación facilitará la organización de su niño/a y reducirá la necesidad de control por parte de usted o de otro adulto.

Sepa cuándo se asignan tareas.
Pregúntele a la maestra o al maestro para estar al tanto de qué tipo de trabajo tendrá que hacer su niño/a y cuándo. Los días que no tenga tareas, su niño/a podría aprovechar ese tiempo para leer.

Prepare un sitio de estudio.
Trate de que su niño/a disponga de un lugar tranquilo y bien iluminado para estudiar. Asegúrese de que haya espacio para libros, papeles, lápices y otros materiales. En el área de estudio no permita distracciones, como la televisión o un aparato de música. Pida que los otros miembros de la familia también colaboren para mantener en silencio el área de trabajo.

Ayude a su niño/a a entender las tareas.
Pídale que tenga preparada una lista de tareas. Aclárele las instrucciones que recibió para realizar el trabajo y, si fuera necesario, déle ejemplos. Luego, conversen sobre cómo su niño/a piensa hacer la tarea.

No haga las tareas de su niño/a.
Su niño/a aprenderá más si hace las tareas de manera independiente, y sentirá la satisfacción de haber hecho las cosas por su cuenta. Si su niño/a no puede completar su trabajo sin ayuda, hable con el maestro o la maestra para ver qué se puede hacer.

Ofrezca su apoyo.
Puede colaborar de las siguientes maneras:

- Ayude a su niño/a a practicar para un examen.

- Asegúrese de que vaya a la biblioteca cuando un proyecto o una tarea lo requiera.

- Muestre interés por las tareas escolares de su niño/a. Pregúntele si quiere que usted las revise.

- Elogie sus progresos.

La adquisición del hábito de hacer las tareas organizadamente será beneficiosa no sólo ahora, sino también en el futuro, cuando su niño/a vaya a los grados superiores y la cantidad de trabajo sea mayor.

Looking at Your Child's Progress

- *How is my child doing in school?*
- *Is my child reading at the right level?*
- *Is my child a good writer?*
- *What can I do to help?*

These are questions that parents often ask.

Report Cards

Report cards are a way of letting parents know how their child is doing in school. Some report cards use letter or number grades. Some include comments from the teacher. Some don't use any grades. Instead, teachers write a paragraph or two describing the progress that the child is making.

The grades and notes on report cards can be based on a variety of things. In addition to test scores, the teacher's observations, samples of the child's work, and the child's own evaluation of his or her work are also taken into account.

Teacher Observation

The teacher is in a position to be a good judge of how your child is progressing. Every day, the teacher observes the learning that is taking place with your child. The teacher can note what the child does well, what the child needs more help with, and how the child is improving. Teachers often keep notes and use checklists of reading and writing behaviors to help them remember what they observe.

Student Self-Assessment

With guidance, children can learn to evaluate their own work. Assessing their own work helps children think about what they have learned and what they still need to know.

Portfolios

When you visit your child's teacher, he or she may show you your child's portfolio. Your child's portfolio will contain materials that have been collected over time, in a systematic way, to show areas of growth as well as areas that need improvement.

A portfolio might include some or all of the following: teacher notes, teacher-completed checklists, tests your child has taken, samples of your child's writing, audiotapes of your child's reading, a reading log that lists books your child has read, and notes your child has made about his or her own work.

By looking at the materials in the portfolio, your child, his or her teacher, and you the parent can see the progress in your child's reading and writing.

What You Can Do

Here are some things you can do to learn more about the methods of assessment used in your child's classroom:

- If you do not understand how your child's teacher evaluates learning, ask the teacher to explain his or her system.

- If your child is discouraged by a grade, explain that learning takes place over time. Ask if he or she knows what to do to improve the grade. If not, make an appointment for you and your child to discuss the grade with the teacher.

- If you are concerned about school performance, don't wait until you are contacted. Make an appointment to talk with your child's teacher. Ask for specific suggestions to help your child improve.

Set high expectations for your child while reminding him or her that everyone has areas of strength and weakness. Always encourage effort, rather than grades. Children need to know that what is most important is that they do their best and keep trying.

Seguimiento del progreso de su niño/a

- *¿Cómo le va a mi niño/a en la escuela?*
- *¿Tiene el nivel de lectura adecuado?*
- *¿Escribe bien?*
- *¿Cómo puedo ayudar a mi niño/a?*

Estas preguntas reflejan algunas cuestiones que suelen preocupar a los padres.

Calificaciones

Por medio de las libretas de calificaciones se informa a los padres sobre el rendimiento de sus hijos en la escuela. Las notas se representan con letras o números; a veces, se incluyen comentarios de los maestros. Algunas escuelas no usan ningún tipo de calificación; en su lugar, los maestros escriben un par de párrafos describiendo el progreso de los estudiantes.

Las notas pueden basarse en diversos factores. Además de la puntuación de los exámenes, también se tienen en cuenta las observaciones de los maestros, los trabajos escritos del estudiante y la autoevaluación del estudiante.

Observaciones de la maestra o del maestro

El maestro o la maestra observa diariamente el proceso de aprendizaje de su niño/a y está en condiciones de evaluar su progreso. Sabe si al estudiante le va bien en la escuela, en qué materias necesita ayuda y qué progresos está haciendo. Los maestros suelen tomar notas y llevar un registro de sus observaciones sobre el nivel de lectura y escritura de cada estudiante.

Autoevaluación

Con una orientación, los estudiantes pueden aprender a evaluar su propio trabajo. Esto les permite reflexionar sobre lo que han aprendido y determinar en qué aspectos necesitan mejorar.

Carpeta del estudiante

Cuando los familiares se entrevistan con los maestros, éstos les enseñan las carpetas de sus hijos, que contienen materiales recogidos de una manera sistemática en lo que va del año escolar y que muestran tanto sus progresos como sus necesidades de mejora.

Una carpeta puede incluir anotaciones y registros de observaciones de los maestros, exámenes, trabajos escritos del estudiante, grabaciones de lecturas del estudiante, un registro de los libros que ha leído y notas de autoevaluación, entre otras cosas.

Observando los materiales de la carpeta usted, su niño/a y el maestro o la maestra podrán evaluar el progreso del estudiante en lectura y escritura.

Cómo puede ayudar

Para comprender mejor los métodos de evaluación empleados en el salón de clases de su niño/a, puede hacer lo siguiente:

- Si no entiende el sistema de evaluación, pídale a la maestra o al maestro que se lo explique.

- Si su niño/a se desanima por una nota, explíquele que el aprendizaje lleva tiempo. Pregúntele si sabe qué puede hacer para mejorar. Si no lo sabe, acompáñelo/la a una entrevista con el maestro o la maestra para conversar sobre el tema.

- Si está preocupado/a por el rendimiento de su niño/a en la escuela, no espere a que el maestro o la maestra se ponga en contacto con usted. Concierte una entrevista y pídale sugerencias específicas para mejorar el nivel de su niño/a.

Establezca unas metas elevadas para su niño/a, pero recuérdele que todos tenemos puntos fuertes y débiles. Elogie siempre el esfuerzo, por encima de las notas obtenidas. Los niños necesitan saber que lo más importante es tratar de hacerlo lo mejor posible y perseverar.

Guiding Your Child's TV Viewing

Have you ever stopped to figure out how much of your child's time is spent watching television? One study estimated that the average child spends more than thirty hours per week viewing television.

You might wonder about the effect that so much TV viewing would have on your child's reading abilities. Studies have shown that watching up to about ten hours per week is slightly beneficial, but watching more than ten hours can have a negative effect on children.

For these reasons, it is important to be aware of the amount of time your child spends in front of the TV set and to make sure that the time spent is as valuable as possible.

Use television to support reading and thinking.

Here are some ideas to help make television work for your child:

- Choose the programs you watch so that you strike a balance of types. Include reading-related programs such as *Reading Rainbow, Long Ago and Far Away,* and *Wonderworks*.

- View programs with your child and discuss them later. Relate the program to your child's own life. Build critical thinking skills. For example, talk about how a character solved a problem. Ask how your child would solve the problem.

- After seeing a show based on a book, read the book. Compare the presentations. Did the TV script differ from the book? How were the characters portrayed? Were the settings the same?

- Replace some commercial entertainment programs with more useful ones. Borrow videos from the library or rent them from a video store.

- After you've watched a program on a particular topic, look in the library for books and articles that will give you and your child more information on the topic.

- Check the library for books related to your child's favorite types of shows. For example, choose books on sporting events, sports, and sports figures.

- Expand your child's interests so that TV must compete with more interesting activities, such as building a model, researching a favorite subject, creating a script, or playing a sport.

- Watch television commercials with your children. Evaluate the claims made for the products sponsors sell. What makes some "new and improved"? Is there any proof that a product works better or tastes the best?

Try these ideas for limiting your child's TV viewing.

- Replace time for TV viewing with reading time.

- Set a maximum number of hours for TV viewing, and help children plan wisely. Use a program guide to decide which programs to watch. In developing your plan, consider your child's favorites as well as programs that will enrich his or her background.

- Build the schedule around homework and chores.

- Follow the schedule. After a specific program is finished, turn the TV off.

- Set a good example by limiting your own television watching.

By guiding your child's TV viewing, you will be helping to make sure that television supports your child's reading experiences.

Orientar a sus niños cómo mirar televisión

¿**S**e ha preguntado alguna vez cuánto tiempo pasa su niño/a mirando televisión? Según un estudio, los niños pasan un promedio de más de treinta horas por semana mirando televisión.

Quizás usted se pregunte qué consecuencias tiene en las destrezas de lectura de su niño/a el pasar tanto tiempo viendo televisión. Algunos estudios han demostrado que mirar unas diez horas de televisión por semana puede ser ligeramente beneficioso, pero que más de diez horas puede tener un efecto negativo en los niños.

Por ello, es importante que usted sepa cuánto tiempo pasa su niño/a mirando televisión y que trate de ayudar a que este tiempo sea lo más productivo posible.

Cómo usar la televisión para reforzar la lectura y el razonamiento

Estas ideas pueden hacer que la televisión sea más beneficiosa para su niño/a:

- Trate de que su niño/a mire programas de varios tipos para mantener un equilibrio. Incluya programas relacionados con libros, como *Reading Rainbow, Long Ago and Far Away* y *Wonderworks.*

- Mire algunos programas con su niño/o y luego, hablen sobre ellos. Busque una conexión entre el programa y la vida de su niño/a. Aliéntele a pensar críticamente. Por ejemplo, conversen sobre lo que hace un personaje para resolver un problema. Después, pregúntele qué solución le daría al problema.

- Después de que su niño/a vea un programa basado en un libro, sugiérale que lea el libro y que los compare. ¿Es el guión televisivo diferente del libro? ¿Cómo se representa a los personajes? ¿Es igual el ambiente?

- Reemplacen los programas de entretenimiento comerciales por otros más beneficiosos. Pidan prestados videos en la biblioteca o alquílenlos.

- Después de mirar un programa interesante, busquen en la biblioteca libros y artículos que les proporcionen más información sobre el tema.

- Busquen en la biblioteca libros relacionados con los temas de los programas preferidos de su niño/a. Por ejemplo, escojan libros sobre eventos deportivos, deportes y deportistas famosos.

- Amplíe los intereses de su niño/a para que la televisión compita con actividades atractivas, como construir un modelo, investigar su tema preferido, crear un guión o practicar un deporte.

- Mire los anuncios comerciales con su niño/a. Evalúen las cualidades que el vendedor reclama para su producto. ¿Qué indicaciones hay de que el producto sea "nuevo y mejor"? ¿Se presenta alguna prueba de que el producto funcione mejor o sea el más sabroso?

Ideas para limitar el tiempo que su niño/a pasa mirando televisión

- Reduzca el tiempo que su niño/a mira televisión y aumente el tiempo de lectura.

- Establezca un tiempo máximo de televisión para su niño/a, y ayúdelo/la a planificarlo inteligentemente. Usen una guía de televisión para seleccionar los programas. Al hacer el plan, consideren tanto los programas preferidos de su niño/a como los que van a aportarle conocimientos.

- Hagan el horario teniendo en cuenta las tareas escolares y otras faenas del hogar.

- Respeten el horario. Cuando el programa termine, apaguen el televisor.

- Dé un buen ejemplo limitando el tiempo que usted ve televisión.

Con su orientación puede lograr que la televisión refuerce las destrezas de lectura de su niño/a.

School's Out!

Learning doesn't stop just because it's vacation time. During the school break, try to find time for a few of the books and activities listed below. They can help your child continue to explore what we studied this year—and get ready for next year!

★= Multicultural

Activities Your Child Can Do Independently

Community Ties
Invite your child to continue to explore community ties. Your child may enjoy
- joining a neighborhood club or team
- helping with a fix-up campaign
- volunteering to walk a neighbor's dog
- gathering outgrown toys or clothes for a local shelter

What's Cooking?
Encourage your child's continued interest in cooking and food. Your child may enjoy
- inventing new sandwiches
- opening a lemonade stand
- comparing the sugar, fat, or salt content of various foods
- planting seeds in a window box or garden

Weather Watch
Your child can continue to explore the weather by
- tracking changes in the weather
- collecting weather lore and testing the accuracy of old stories
- recording record highs and lows on a map of the United States
- watching clouds

Activities You and Your Child Can Enjoy Together

Disaster!
Discuss safety precautions before you do any hiking, camping, or swimming. Form a plan in case someone gets lost or separated from the group.

Community Ties
As you visit nearby communities or travel long distances, share observations with your child. How is the new town like your own? What differences seem most striking?

Building Common Ground
You and your child have much in common. Enjoy activities that are fun for both of you. Develop new interests by
- planning an activity together
- teaching one another how to do something
- learning a new craft or hobby
- discussing books, movies, and TV programs

Reading Suggestions

★*Angel Child, Dragon Child* by Michelle Maria Surat. Scholastic 1989 (40p)

Beverly Cleary: She Makes Reading Fun by Patricia S. Martin. Rourke 1987 (32p)

The Case of the Happy Stranger by Crosby Bonsall. HarperCollins 1995 (32p) *Available in Spanish.*

★*Donovan's Word Jar* by Monalisa DeGross. HarperCollins 1994 (71p)

Eagle by Judy Allen. Candlewick 1994 (26p)

Grandfather's Pencil and the Room of Stories by Michael Foreman. Harcourt 1994 (32p)

Home Place by Crescent Dragonwagon. Macmillan 1990 (32p)

The Jellybean Principal by Catherine McMorrow. Random 1994 (48p)

Koko's Kitten by Dr. Francine Patterson. Scholastic 1985 (32p)

The Lucky Baseball Bat by Matt Christopher. Little Brown 1991 (58p)

★*Making a New Home in America* by Maxine Rosenberg and George Ancona. Lothrop 1986 (48p)

Mirette on the High Wire by Emily Arnold McCully. Putnam 1992 (32p) *Available in Chinese.*

My First Green Book by Angela Wilkes. Knopf 1991 (48p) *Available in Spanish.*

Nate the Great and the Musical Note by Marjorie Winman Sharmat. Putnam 1990 (48p)

A New England Scrapbook by Loretta Krupinski. HarperCollins 1994 (40p)

Sea Lion by Caroline Arnold. Morrow 1994 (48p)

The Seven Treasure Hunts by Betsy Byars. HarperCollins 1991 (74p)

Silver at Night by Susan Campbell Bartoletti. Crown 1994 (32p)

¡Se acabó el año escolar!

Durante las vacaciones no se deja de aprender. En esta época, traten de hallar el tiempo para leer algunos de los libros o actividades mencionados en la siguiente lista. Estos ayudarán a su niño/a a continuar explorando las cosas que aprendimos durante el año escolar y a prepararse para el siguiente año.

★= Multicultural

Actividades independientes para su niño/a

Nuestra comunidad

Pídanle a su niño/a que siga explorando los lazos con la comunidad. Tal vez disfrute de lo siguiente:

- asociarse a un club o equipo del vecindario
- ayudar en una campaña de embellecer el vecindario
- ofrecer pasear el perro de un vecino
- juntar juguetes o ropa que ya no se use para un refugio cercano

¡Buen provecho!

Animen a su niño/a a que continúe interesándose por las comidas y la cocina. Tal vez disfrute de lo siguiente:

- inventar nuevos tipos de sándwiches o tacos
- abrir un puesto de venta de limonada
- plantar semillas en un macetero o en un jardín
- comparar el contenido de azúcar, grasas o sal de varios alimentos

¿Qué tiempo hace?

Pídanle a su niño/a que continúe observando el tiempo

- anotando cambios en el tiempo
- juntando dichos antiguos sobre el tiempo y verificando si son ciertos
- anotando récords de temperaturas máximas y mínimas en un mapa de los Estados Unidos
- observando las nubes

Actividades para hacer juntos

¡Desastre!

Hablen de precauciones de seguridad antes de que salgan a caminar por la montaña, o vayan a acampar o a nadar. Decidan qué harán si alguien se pierde o se separa del grupo.

Nuestra comunidad

Cuando visiten vecindarios cercanos o viajen a lugares distantes, compartan observaciones con su niño/a. ¿En qué se parece el nuevo lugar al lugar donde viven? ¿Cuáles son las diferencias que más se notan?

Construir una base en común

Ustedes y su niño/a tienen mucho en común. Realicen actividades que ustedes y su niño/a disfrutan. Adquieran nuevos intereses de la siguiente manera:

- Decidan juntos qué actividad llevar a cabo.
- Enséñense unos a otros a hacer algo.
- Aprendan una nueva artesanía o pasatiempo.
- Hablen de libros, películas y programas de TV.

Sugerencias de lecturas para las vacaciones

★*Angel Child, Dragon Child* por Michelle Maria Surat. Scholastic

Beverly Cleary: Hace divertida la lectura por Patricia S. Martin. Rourke

El caso de forastero hambriento por Crosby Bonsall. Harper Arco Iris

★*Donovan's Word Jar* por Monalisa DeGross. HarperCollins 1994 (71p)

Eagle por Judy Allen. Candlewick 1994 (26p)

Grandfather's Pencil and the Room of Stories por Michael Foreman. Harcourt 1994 (32p)

Home Place por Crescent Dragonwagon. Macmillan 1990 (32p)

The Jellybean Principal por Catherine McMorrow. Random 1994 (48p)

Koko's Kitten por Dr. Francine Patterson. Scholastic 1985 (32p)

The Lucky Baseball Bat por Matt Christopher. Little Brown

★*Making a New Home in America* por Maxine Rosenberg y George Ancona. Lothrop 1986 (48p)

Mi primer libro de ecología por Angela Wilkes. Lectorum

Mirette on the High Wire por Emily Arnold McCully. Putnam 1992 (32p)

Nate the Great and the Musical Note por Marjorie Winman Sharmat. Putnam 1990 (48p)

A New England Scrapbook por Loretta Krupinski. HarperCollins 1994 (40p)

Sea Lion por Caroline Arnold. Morrow 1994 (48p)

The Seven Treasure Hunts por Betsy Byars. HarperCollins 1991 (74p)

Silver at Night por Susan Campbell Bartoletti. Crown 1994

Using Volunteers in the Classroom

Section Three of ***Home/Community Connections*** provides ideas and materials to help you work with volunteers in the classroom. Besides general information on using volunteers, this section includes forms for inviting and thanking them. There is also a list of specific volunteer topics related to your themes and a handbook for volunteers with general information about volunteering, special requests for bilingual volunteers and volunteer coordinators, and directions for accomplishing specific tasks in the classroom. Select those materials and ideas that are appropriate to your style of teaching and your classroom. Similar forms and information on the Teacher's Resource Disk are indicated with an icon.

💻 = Teacher's Resource Disks

TABLE OF CONTENTS FOR SECTION 3

Introduction _____ 88
    Using Volunteers in the Classroom
    Tips and Guidelines for Using Volunteers
    Identifying Volunteers
    Providing Information for Volunteers
    Managing Volunteers in the Classroom
    Related Reading

💻 **Request for Volunteers** _____ 90

💻 **Volunteer Topics** _____ 91

Volunteer Handbook
    Volunteer Handbook (Cover and General Information) _____ 93
    Reading Aloud to Students _____ 94
    Listening to a Student Read _____ 95
    Sharing Books _____ 96
    Helping Students Select Books _____ 97
    Making a Book _____ 98
    Bilingual Volunteers _____ 99
    Being a Volunteer at Home _____ 100
    Volunteer Coordinators _____ 101

Volunteer Certificate _____ 102

Using Volunteers in the Classroom

If you have decided you would like to use volunteers in the classroom, the next thing to consider is how best to make use of their support. You can use volunteers to provide:

- **background and enrichment.** Volunteers can talk to the class about experiences related to the reading themes, and share information about their work, hobbies, interests, or knowledge of a culture or a country. They can also contribute to the classroom environment by helping with theme bulletin boards and displays, by taking charge of a center or long-term project, and by contributing knowledge about the cultural diversity of your school.

- **practice and reinforcement.** Volunteers can add to the one-on-one and small-group practice and reinforcement so valuable to students' progress. They can read to children, listen to children read individually or in small groups, discuss stories, take dictation from younger children, help older children check and revise their writing, review vocabulary and spelling lists, listen to a child's presentation before it's

presented to the class, and assist with any number of other things.

- **support.** Volunteers can provide other kinds of support for you and children as well, such as making audiotapes of stories, donating or organizing materials for class projects, typing children's work for a class display, newsletter, or literary booklet, and performing any other helpful task in the classroom or at home.

- **communication.** Volunteers who speak a language other than English can help you communicate with children and parents who speak that language by phone, during conferences, at school functions, within the classroom, and for non-English-speaking parents who want to be involved in the classroom by demonstrating a skill or a craft.

As you consider the topics and tasks outlined in this section, you'll have your own ideas of how best to use volunteers in the classroom. If there is not a volunteer coordinator for your school, you may also wish to elicit the help of a parent volunteer to help you coordinate your volunteer program.

Tips and Guidelines for Using Volunteers

Check school policies. Your school may have policies regarding non-staff participation in the classroom. These policies may determine:

- **who can volunteer.** Parents, grandparents, other relatives, members of the community, high school or college students? Are there any restrictions? For example, are parents permitted to work with their own children? in the same classroom?

- **management procedures.** Are volunteers handled by the classroom teacher or by a school coordinator? If your school has a volunteer coordinator, you will want to check with that person to see what the requirements are, what forms are in use, and which additional forms provided in this section might also be used.

Provide clear instructions. Volunteers will be more confident and more effective if they know exactly what they are doing and when. Confirm

dates and times with volunteers. You may also need to provide clear written as well as verbal instructions for the tasks you plan for volunteers. (See the Volunteer Handbook on pages 93–101 of this section.) Encourage volunteers to ask questions and come to you for help, if necessary.

Prepare for any problems that may arise. Plan for supervision by a teacher or other education professional of any volunteer who works directly with students. Then explain your classroom rules to volunteers, and provide guidelines for dealing with students' behavioral problems. You might:

- share your techniques for handling disputes and discipline problems.

- advise your volunteers to return a child to your group if there is a problem.

Show your appreciation. Let volunteers know you appreciate their help. Discuss with volunteers (immediately or later) how each task went, and offer support and encouragement as needed.

Identifying Volunteers

Request for Volunteers This form, on page 90, can be used to enlist the aid of parents in the classroom and to identify those parents who wish to volunteer. You might distribute the form at an Open House or Back-to-School Night. Or, send it home with children at the beginning of the school year. If your school authorizes other volunteers in the classroom, the form can also be used to invite them to help out. Note that the form includes a place for volunteers to identify themselves as possible interpreters who can help communicate with children and/or parents who speak a native language other than English.

Volunteer Topics This list of topics, on page 91, can be distributed along with the Request for Volunteers. The topics reflect the themes you will cover in the reading program, giving examples of theme-related information volunteers can present to your class for the purposes of background building or extension.

Providing Information for Volunteers

Volunteer Handbook The Volunteer Handbook (pages 93–101) includes general information on volunteering, along with information sheets that identify and explain various tasks and activities volunteers (including bilingual volunteers) can carry out to help you and your class. Some or all of the Volunteer Handbook can be photocopied and then stapled to make individual copies for parents, or placed in a binder and sent home to parents on a rotating basis.

Together, the Request for Volunteers, the Volunteer Topics list, and the Volunteer Handbook will let potential volunteers know what they might do.

Volunteer Certificate The simple certificate on page 102 can be completed and sent to your volunteers as a way to acknowledge their contribution and thank them for helping out. It includes space for children to sign their names, adding to the rewarding experience for both volunteer and children.

Managing Volunteers in the Classroom

Volunteer Coordinators In some schools, home-school or volunteer coordinators oversee parent and community volunteers. In others, teachers manage the volunteers. In either case, a classroom volunteer coordinator can help you organize and manage your volunteers. Such coordinators can also be used on a per project basis to manage more detailed activities that involve several volunteers or require more planning. The Volunteer Coordinators topic on page 101 of the Volunteer Handbook suggests ways in which coordinators might benefit your class.

Related Reading

"The Dos and Don'ts of Using Parent Volunteers," Linda Shalaway. *Instructor,* July/August 1994, p. 78. Teachers and volunteers offer fourteen tips for successful parent involvement and six pitfalls to avoid.

The Volunteer Tutor's Toolbox, Beth Ann Herrmann, ed. International Reading Association, 1994. Education professionals provide practical ideas for volunteers who tutor learners of all ages.

Our Classroom Needs Your Help!

We are looking for volunteers to help both in and out of the classroom. General help, such as reading aloud to students, helping with class projects, or preparing materials at home, is always welcome. In addition, we need people who can share their knowledge and experience on topics we will learn about this year. If you would like to help, please fill out the form below and return it to school. If you can help, I will contact you to make arrangements. Thank you!

Name: _____

Relationship to Student: _____

Phone Number: _____

Please take a few moments to tell me about yourself:

Talents _____

Interests _____

Hobbies _____

Collections _____

Job _____

Knowledge of countries/cultures _____

❑ I can spend some time every week working with students in the classroom.

  Days Available _____

  Times Available _____

❑ I cannot come to school every week, but I can come once or maybe a few times.

❑ I cannot come to school, but I would like to help by doing things at home.

❑ I speak a language other than English. I speak _____

❑ I would be willing to work with a student who speaks this language.

❑ I would be willing to translate for parents who speak this language.

❑ I would like to help but cannot at this time. Please contact me later.

Some Special Topics for Volunteers

Listed below are some of the topics we will be studying this year. Please indicate any topic that you would be willing to share information about. Just check the topic(s) and fill in your name and phone number at the bottom of the page. If you wish, write a brief description of your topic on the back of this sheet. Return it to school. One or two weeks before we study a topic you've indicated, I will call to see if you are available to come in and share your knowledge with the class. Thanks for your help!

Thanks for your help!

❏ **Oink, Oink, Oink** Are you willing to share with us a folktale, legend, or song about pigs? Can you help us learn more about pigs, wolves, and sharks? Would you be interested in explaining to us how a house is built or in teaching us how to read a blueprint? Have you ever lived in or visited a desert? Hawaii?

❏ **Community Ties** Are you a community official, such as a mayor, a city councilor, a or town planner? Have you lived in our community for a long time and observed the way it has changed over the years? Can you share with us how our community is both similar to and different from others you have known? Would you be willing to teach us a song, a story, or a custom that is important to you and your family?

❏ **Disaster!** The disasters we will explore include the sinking of the *Titanic*, volcanic eruptions like the one in ancient Pompeii, and the molasses explosion in Boston. Do you know anything about these or other disasters? Do you know any songs or stories about disasters that you can share with us?

❏ **What's Cooking?** Would you be willing to make a favorite dish for an international food festival? Are you interested in helping us cook or sharing how you first learned to cook? Are you an expert on nutrition? Do you speak Italian or Ukrainian? Do you know songs or folktales from either culture or from some other part of the world?

❏ **Weather Watch** Are you a professional or amateur meteorologist? Do you provide emergency help as part of your job? Do you work in a weather-related industry? Do you know a story about a tornado, hurricane, or other weather emergency that you can share with us? Do you know any weather-related songs, folktales, or legends?

❏ **What a Day!** Are you willing to share your memories of a holiday your family observes or a special day in your life? One of the stories we will read focuses on a special haircut. Do you have stories of memorable, funny, or disastrous haircuts? Another story features a train. Could you tell us about trains or recall a train ride that you took? We will also be exploring a day in the life of a veterinarian. Would you be willing to share with us what your work day is like?

Name _____

Phone Number _____

Volunteer Handbook

Included in this handbook is information about some of the different kinds of activities that you as a classroom volunteer may be asked to do. In addition, here are some general tips that will help you be an effective and valuable volunteer.

- *Be on time.* The students' learning activities are carefully scheduled. Being even ten minutes late can disrupt the scheduling of other classes and activities.

- *Let the teacher know about cancellations.* The teacher should be informed of cancellations at least 24 hours in advance of the scheduled visit.

- *Leave younger children at home.* School seems like a natural place to bring children, but younger children need attention and supervision. In the busy atmosphere of a classroom, they can become especially excited.

- *Respect students' rights by treating their learning and behavior in a confidential manner.* The classroom is a protected environment for learning. It is important not to discuss students' abilities or actions in the classroom with others.

- *Feel free to ask for help.* If you are not sure how to proceed with what you have been asked to do, or if you are having any difficulties, feel free to ask questions or to ask for help from the teacher.

Reading Aloud to Students

Students of all ages enjoy having someone read aloud to them. One of the best things about reading to students is that it gets them interested in and excited about reading. It motivates them to read on their own. Here are some ways to generate attention and interest in a book you are reading aloud.

Prepare for your reading.
Read the book yourself before you read it to students. (If possible, do this at home.) You will be able to make the selection more interesting to your listeners if you are familiar with it. If you have not read aloud to a group before, you may want to practice reading the selection aloud.

Read with expression.
To add interest to your reading, make your facial expressions and voice match what's happening in the story.

Keep eye contact with your audience.
From time to time, look up from your reading to make eye contact with students. Maintaining frequent eye contact helps draw the listeners into the story.

Engage your listeners.
Pause from time to time to ask students what they think will happen next in a story, or what they think about what has happened so far. Encourage students to comment on the information in nonfiction books, and to ask questions about what you are reading.

Show any pictures.
Pictures add to the enjoyment of a book. If you're reading a picture book, hold the book to the side as you read. If the book you're reading has just a few pictures in it, show each picture before or after reading the page.

Don't read too fast.
Remember that students are using their imaginations to picture what you read. If you are a fast reader, make an effort to slow down.

Discuss the selection.
Ask students what they thought about the selection. Did they like how it ended? Which character did they like best? What was their favorite part? the funniest part? the saddest part? What *didn't* they like about it? When you are reading informational books, ask students to share something they learned.

Listening to a Student Read

First, identify what book the student will read. Find out from the classroom teacher how the book is to be selected—by the teacher, by the student, or by you and the student together. Then, here are some things you can do to provide the student with a worthwhile experience.

Convey a positive attitude.
Let the student know that you are glad to be there and that you look forward to hearing the selection he or she will read to you.

Show interest in the book.
Look at the cover together, and flip through the pages. Encourage the student to comment on anything of interest, such as what the book might be about or what he or she expects to learn.

Help the student handle an unfamiliar word.
Avoid frustration and maintain interest in the selection by making the process of figuring out a word short and simple. Have the student skip the word and read to the end of the sentence. Then go back and ask what word would make sense in the sentence. Ask what word parts the student knows. Then ask what letter sounds the student knows. If there are pictures, see if they provide a clue. If the word is still unknown, simply pronounce it for the student.

Discuss the book.
Talk about the selection. Discuss what each of you liked or disliked about it and why.

Review difficult words.
Look back through the book at any words that were important to the selection and that gave the student difficulty. Discuss the words and their meanings.

Give encouragement.
Comment on something the student did well, such as how many words the student knew, the way the student figured out a word, or how much better the student is reading since the last time you heard him or her read.

Sharing Books

Students enjoy reading books over and over again. They particularly enjoy reading their favorite selections to an adult or a friend. Here are some effective techniques you can use when listening to small groups read.

For reading any selection:
- Have one group read the story aloud together while the other group listens. Then have the first group listen while the second group reads.

- Ask each student to locate and read the funniest, most exciting, or most interesting part of a selection. Have students explain why they chose those parts.

- Have students take turns reading parts of the story aloud as you record them on an audiotape. Play back the tape, and have the group suggest ways that each student's reading could be improved. Then, as students take turns rereading the text, have the other students point out the improvements.

For reading selections that include dialogue:
- Assign different students to read the part of each character. Have the rest of the group read aloud the other parts.

For reading informational selections:
- Have students take turns reading a portion of the selection aloud. Have the other students in the group close their books and listen to the reading as one might listen to a radio broadcast. Following the reading, have the listeners summarize what was read. If any portion was unclear, students can open their books, locate the portion in question, and reread it.

For reading poetry:
- Have students read the poem in unison.
- Have different students or parts of the group read different lines or stanzas.

Before deciding which techniques to use, read the selection aloud yourself. Decide which techniques would work best for the selection. If you are unsure of which techniques to use, ask the teacher. Or, give students the options and ask *how they* would like to read the selection.

Helping Students Select Books

Reading can open doors to interesting worlds. But finding a great book is not always easy. Here are some things you can do to help.

Identify students' interests.
Help students figure out what kinds of books they would enjoy. Ask about kinds of books: adventure, mystery, fairy tales, fantasy, humor. Ask about the students' hobbies, pets, favorite movies, sports, and after-school activities. Then help students look for stories or nonfiction selections that reflect these special interests. Encourage students to ask the teacher or librarian for books about specific topics, too.

Expand on students' interests.
Once you get to know students, point out subjects related to those in which they have expressed interest. Suggest that students look for books on these topics, as well as for other books by authors of stories they have enjoyed.

Have students preview books.
Urge students to read the inside flap of the book jacket or the beginning pages to see whether a book will hold their interest.

Determine whether students can read the book.
The "five finger method" is a simple way to find out if a book is at the right reading level for a student. Have the student read the first page of the book, holding up a finger for each word he or she comes to that is unfamiliar. If there are five words on the page that the student doesn't know, the book is probably too hard; however, leave the final decision on whether to read the book to the student. If the student is really interested in the book, he or she can probably read it with support, and enjoy it.

Making a Book

When students are ready to "publish," or share, their writings, help them follow these directions to make a book.

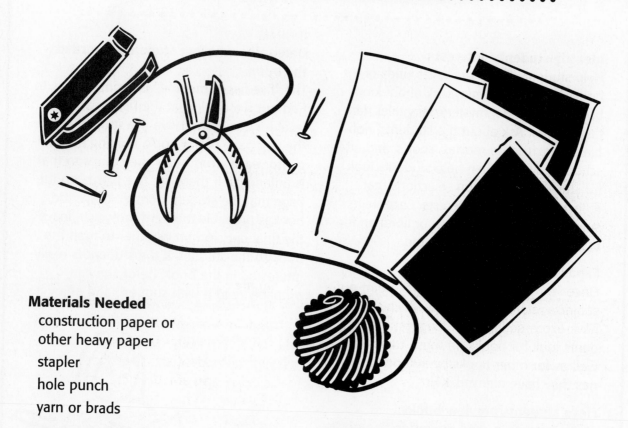

Materials Needed
construction paper or
other heavy paper
stapler
hole punch
yarn or brads

1. Make the cover.
Each student can pick one of these ways to make a cover:

• Use two sheets of paper—one for the front cover and one for the back cover.

• Fold a large piece of construction paper in half.

2. Design the front cover.
Have each student write his or her name and the title on the cover. Suggest that they draw pictures on the covers or decorate them in some other way.

3. Bind the book.
Remind students to number their pages before they put them inside the cover. Then help them bind the books in one of these ways:

• Have students who are using a two-piece cover punch three holes through the cover and pages, and insert yarn or brads to hold the book together.

• Help students who are using a folded cover to staple the entire book together in three places along the spine.

Bilingual Volunteers

We need your special skills very much. Here are some things you might be asked to do:

- **Make telephone calls.** You might be asked to call families to let them know what's going on at school, to set up conference dates, to find out their concerns and questions, and to ask questions for me.

- **Translate when parents come to school.** We don't want anyone to feel ignored or to miss out on important information. You might be asked to translate at parent-teacher conferences, when a parent comes to demonstrate a skill or craft to the class, at school meetings, or at any of the school's social functions.

- **Translate written materials.** We have many forms, letters, newsletters, and other information traveling between school and home. It would be very helpful to have these materials translated for parents who do not speak English.

- **Translate for a child.** Some children may need to have instructions or assignments translated. Also, there may be times when children present oral reports to the class. Depending on a child's English proficiency, you might help translate the child's work so that he or she can present it in class, or the child might give the presentation in his or her home language as you translate for the class.

- **Read aloud.** You can read aloud to children in their own language. We also need help *finding* suitable books for children in languages other than English.

General Tips

Here are some suggestions that will help you make all families feel they are an important part of our school community:

- Do your best to put family members at ease. This may not be easy, especially if they have had difficulty communicating with a school due to language differences before. It may help to explain that you are also a parent (rather than a school official) and that you have volunteered to serve as a contact for them because you speak their language.

- If you are acting as a translator for a family at school, be sure to arrive before they do so that they can speak with someone immediately upon their arrival.

- Maintain confidentiality at all times. The information you are relaying is, of course, usually handled by a school official. It is crucial that a family's privacy be respected.

- If you are comfortable doing so, you can give your telephone number to the family. Then if they have a question or a problem, they can contact you.

- If you can help us put families in contact with other community members who speak their language, please let us know. Some families may have ample contact with their community and extended family. However, if the family is new to our area, any helpful hints for putting them in contact with special stores, services, and associations would be appreciated.

Being a Volunteer at Home

A full-time job outside the home, lack of transportation, small children at home—there are many reasons why you may not be able to serve as a volunteer in the classroom. Still, there are a variety of ways you can help from your home. Here are a few examples of things you can do:

Prepare art materials.
The teacher might have you trace and cut items from construction paper, or prepare cardboard patterns that students can use for tracing.

Type students' stories.
Students may need to have the stories they write typed for classroom publishing. Check how much text to put on each page. Verify whether you should make any corrections in grammar, punctuation, or spelling. You might also transcribe students' oral stories from tape.

Bind students' writings into books.
This handbook includes simple instructions for making books of students' writings. You can follow the directions to make the books at home, decorating the covers yourself or sending the covered books to school to be decorated by the students.

Repair paperback books.
Paperback books tear easily, and students' favorites from the classroom library are always in need of repair.

Help with refreshments for a special event.
You can bake cookies or prepare other food or drinks.

If you are going to be an at-home volunteer, it is important to find out:

- **how to obtain the materials.** Do you need to come to school to get them, or can the teacher send them to you?

- **exact instructions.** Make sure you clearly understand what you are being asked to do. Ask questions. Once you get started, if you have more questions, don't hesitate to call the teacher for help.

- **when the teacher needs the job completed.** What is your deadline, and how will the materials be returned to school?

Volunteer Coordinators

Volunteers are important and have much to offer children, but they also need supervision and management. I need one or more people to help organize and manage the many volunteers who have so generously offered their time. Here are some things a volunteer coordinator may be asked to do:

Maintain a volunteer schedule. You can help me create monthly calendars to show who has volunteered and when they will come to school. One or two days before a volunteer is due to help, you might make a reminder telephone call.

Manage a project. Some of the projects planned for the year involve several volunteers. As coordinator for a single project, you might meet with volunteers to decide who will do tasks and when they are due.

Oversee special events. For special events, such as theme celebrations, holiday parties, and Back-to-School Night, you as coordinator, might call on volunteers asking them to supply treats or donate paper goods.

Find volunteers for field trips. Chaperones are always needed for school trips and other outings. As coordinator for a field trip, you might be asked to call parents to get some to chaperone.

Line up volunteers for theme units. As the class begins a new theme, you might call parents who expressed an interest in this theme to see if they are still able to help. Then, we can work together to set up a schedule that meets the needs of the volunteers and the children.

Manage at-home volunteers. As coordinator, you might make sure volunteers who want to work from home have the materials and instructions they need to complete their tasks. You might also assist by delivering or picking up materials at their homes.

General Tips

- **Know your task.** Make sure you understand what your role as coordinator involves. If you have any questions about what you should do, ask me for help. I appreciate your time.

- **Identify yourself.** When you telephone a volunteer, make sure he or she knows who you are. It might help to mention my name or the name of the school to help the volunteer understand the nature of the call.

- **Work as a team.** Remember, the people you are managing are volunteers who have offered their time because they really want to help. Make use of your volunteers and work as a team. Don't try to do all the work yourself.

- **Meet as a group.** If you are working with several volunteers for a specific project or a special event, try to meet as a group at least once.

- **Offer support.** Make sure volunteers know where to reach you if they have questions.

Volunteer Certificate

This is to certify that

_____

helped our class by

_____

We think you're great!

_____

(date)

_____

(teacher)

and the class:

_____ _____

_____ _____

_____ _____

_____ _____

_____ _____

_____ _____

_____ _____

_____ _____

Moving Beyond the Classroom

Section Four of **Home/Community Connections** provides information and ideas you can use to start a number of different programs involving families and the community, or to expand programs you already have in place. Included are materials to help you start a family reading program, conduct a workshop, start a Homework Club for students, set up a resource center for parents, and even search out people and businesses in the community that can help you and your students. Similar forms and information on the Teacher's Resource Disks are indicated with an icon.

❖ = Appears in English and Spanish

🖥 = Teacher's Resource Disks

TABLE OF CONTENTS FOR SECTION 4

A Family Reading Program _____ 104
❖ Reading Contract _____ 107
Parent Book List _____ 109
Sharing Family Stories _____ 111
Conducting a Workshop _____ 113
Setting Up a Parent Resource Center _____ 115
Working with the Community _____ 117
Starting a Homework Club _____ 119
Assessing Your Home/Community Program _____ 120

A Family Reading Program

Numerous research studies have indicated that reading together is the single most effective way parents can contribute to their children's success in school. One way to structure this type of parent involvement is to implement a Family Reading Program. A Family Reading Program is a program in which families commit to spending a specific amount of time each week reading and discussing books together.

Planning the Program

There are several ways to set up a Family Reading Program. You can implement a school-wide program or an individual classroom program. Sometimes the best plan results from modifying a school-wide program to suit the needs of each class. Choose the plan that is most appropriate for your school community.

How Much Time?

Depending on the participants, reading programs have different expectations. In general, programs ask families to commit to spending 15 to 20 minutes, 3 to 5 days a week reading together. Parents' work schedules and students' after-school commitments may influence this decision.

Family Involvement

To accommodate busy schedules and different levels of literacy, most programs suggest a variety of ways of fulfilling the reading time:

- The parent or another family member can read to the child.
- The child can read to the parent or another family member.
- The parent or other family member and the child can listen to a recording of someone else reading.
- The reading may be done in English or a different primary language.

Getting a Commitment to Family Reading

There are a variety of ways of helping to ensure commitment to a Family Reading Program. Here are a few ways you might try:

- Sometimes families sign copies of a contract such as the Reading Contract, provided in English and Spanish on pages 107 and 108.
- Some families keep logs of the material read, the number of minutes spent reading each day, and comments on their experience.
- Some programs encourage the reading of one of four or five books pre-selected by all families. Periodically, the families will meet at school or in a family's home for an evening of refreshments and book discussion.

Choosing Materials

Books and other materials for home reading can come from a variety of sources:

- the classroom library, using a check-out system
- the school library or learning center
- the public library

- school-sponsored book sales
- local, state, or federally funded reading incentive programs, such as RIF (Reading is Fundamental)
- books in the home
- newspapers, magazines, and newsletters

The Parent Book List on page 109 can be used to help parents choose appropriate books.

Besides print materials, audiotapes are available from some of the same sources. The Houghton Mifflin *Invitations to Literacy* audiotapes can be sent home (with a tape player, if necessary) on a rotating basis.

For families acquiring English, try to provide books and other print materials in their first language. Encourage families who come from cultures with strong oral traditions to share their stories by recording them. Students might write the stories down in the home language and/or translate them into English to share with others.

Launching the Program

Simple planning can ensure a successful launch of your program. Create interest and excitement by providing information and resources for parents. Have students make flyers to take home to spark parents' interest. Send a brief letter home to parents explaining the program. Or, take advantage of a Back-to-School Night or Open House to talk to parents in person. You might also offer a workshop to orient families to the Family Reading Program. The information in this manual on Conducting a Workshop (pages 113 and 114) can help you prepare.

Incentives and Rewards

Some schools offer incentives to families to involve as many as possible. (However, you may find that once family reading becomes a habit, no other incentives are needed!) The following are some rewards and incentives that some schools have found successful:

- Present a book to students who complete a reading program. Your school's Parent Teacher Association may be able to help with the purchase of books.
- Award certificates of accomplishment to families at the close of the year.
- Hold a banquet to honor families who participate.
- Start an "ice cream club." When a certain number of families have kept their commitment for a predetermined number of weeks, an ice cream party is held. (Of course, you could substitute another treat.)

However you choose to do it, a Family Reading Program is sure to foster student learning and family cohesiveness.

Related Reading

"Encouraging independent reading through the reading millionaires project," Gail A. O'Masta and James M. Wolf. *The Reading Teacher*, Vol. 44, No. 9, May 1991, p. 656. An elementary school in Panama initiates "The Reading Millionaires Project," which sets a school-wide goal for students of reading a million minutes outside the classroom.

"The Partnership for Family Reading: Benefits for families and schools," Ruth D. Handel. *The Reading Teacher*, Vol. 46, No. 2, October 1992, p. 116. Family literacy programs provide learning experiences that benefit adults as well as children.

"To Home and Back with Books," Min Hong. *Instructor*, September 1995, p. 64. A first-grade teacher in New York City explains how to manage a highly successful home reading program.

Additional references are available through the Houghton Mifflin/GNN Education Center, a free online service located on the Internet. Access the Education Center through the School Division Home Page on Houghton Mifflin's World Wide Web site. The URL address: **http://www.hmco.com/school/**

READING CONTRACT

We agree to spend 15 minutes reading together at least 3 nights a week.

Sometimes we will take turns reading aloud to each other, and sometimes just one of us will read aloud.

We will reread books that we like and want to share with each other, or we will choose new books to explore together.

_____

(Child)

_____

(Parent or Other Reader)

Parents: Please sign the contract and have your child sign it, too. You may find it helpful to keep track of your reading time by marking on a calendar every day you spend 15 minutes reading together.

CONTRATO DE LECTURA

Estamos de acuerdo en leer 15 minutos juntos, al menos 3 noches por semana.

Leeremos en voz alta; unas veces nos turnaremos y otras leerá uno de los dos.

Volveremos a leer libros que nos hayan gustado y cuya lectura queramos compartir, o elegiremos nuevos libros para explorarlos juntos.

_____
(Estudiante)

_____
(Padre, madre o tutor)

Padre/Madre/Tutor: Por favor, firme el contrato y pídale a su hijo/a que lo firme también. Podría serle de utilidad llevar la cuenta del tiempo que leen haciendo marcas en un calendario cada vez que lean 15 minutos juntos.

Parent Book List

These books were specially selected as children's favorites. You may want to discuss the contents of the books to see which ones your child is interested in. These books should be available at your local library. You might want to ask the librarian for assistance or for further recommendations.

• •

★= Multicultural

Abel's Island by William Steig. Farrar 1976 (119p) During a storm, a gentleman mouse is accidentally separated from his wife and must learn to survive on an island. *Available in Spanish as* La isla de Abel.

A Bear Called Paddington by Michael Bond. Houghton 1958 (128p) When Mr. and Mrs. Brown find a bear wearing a sign reading "please look after this bear," they welcome him into their family. (See others in the series.)

★*The Contest: An Armenian Folktale* by Nonny Hogrogian. Greenwillow 1976 (32p) Two robbers courting the same girl decide on a contest to see who will marry her.

A Cricket in Times Square by George Selden. Farrar 1960 Chester Cricket, Harry the Cat, and Tucker Mouse join forces to help the Bellini family save their newsstand in Times Square. (See others in the series.) *Available in Spanish as* Un grillo en Times Square.

Dinosaur Bob and His Adventures with the Family Lazardo by William Joyce. HarperCollins 1988 (32p) The Lazardo family returns from Africa with a dinosaur named Bob, who learns to play baseball.

Granny, Will Your Dog Bite? and Other Mountain Rhymes by Gerald Milnes. Knopf 1990 (45p) A collection of riddles, spelling rhymes, nonsense rhymes, and stories from Appalachia.

Hailstones and Halibut Bones: Adventures in Color by Mary O'Neill. Doubleday 1961 (64p) This classic collection presents twelve rich and vivid poems that describe colors and how they make one feel.

Heidi by Joanna Spyri. Puffin 1983 (240p) (Other editions are also available.) In this well-loved classic, a little girl is sent to live with her grandfather in the Alps. *Available in Spanish as* Heidi.

Her Seven Brothers by Paul Goble. Bradbury 1988 (32p) This Cheyenne legend explains the creation of the Big Dipper.

★*Hmong Folk Tales 1 and 2* edited by Charles Johnson. Shen 1980 (28p) This collection presents traditional Hmong folktales. *Text in English/Hmong.*

★*Honey, I Love and Other Love Poems* by Eloise Greenfield. HarperCollins 1978 (48p) This collection of poems celebrates the joys of childhood.

★*How Many Spots Does a Leopard Have and Other Tales* by Julius Lester. Scholastic 1989 (72p) This collection presents twelve African and Jewish folktales.

Ida Early Comes Over the Mountain by Robert Burch. Puffin 1990 (160p) (Other editions are also available.) Life takes a humorous turn for the four motherless Sutton children and their father when Ida shows up to keep house for them.

★*John Henry* by Julius Lester. Dial 1994 (40p) The classic American folktale of man against machine is retold by a master storyteller.

Just So Stories by Rudyard Kipling. HarperCollins 1991 (128p) Twelve pourquoi tales from Kipling include stories about how the camel got his hump and how the alphabet was invented.

The King's Equal by Katherine Paterson. HarperCollins 1992 (64p) Prince Raphael is ordered by his dying father to find a bride who is the prince's equal in all ways, and his search brings surprising results.

The *Little House* books by Laura Ingalls Wilder. HarperCollins 1953 (336p) Beginning with *Little House on the Prairie*, this series chronicles the lives of Laura, Mary, Ma and Pa Ingalls during the 1800s. (See others in the series.) *Many of the* Little House *books are available in Spanish.*

★*Lon Po Po: A Red Riding Hood Story From China* by Ed Young. Philomel 1989 (32p) This dramatic version of the European Red Riding Hood story was awarded the Caldecott Medal for its illustrations. *Available in Chinese.*

Mr. Popper's Penguins by Florence and Richard Atwater. Little, Brown 1938 (139p) Mr. Popper finds himself raising a family of penguins, which he trains to perform and then takes on the road.

Mrs. Piggle-Wiggle by Betty MacDonald. HarperCollins 1957 (119p) Mrs. Piggle-Wiggle has a cure for every childhood ailment, including her old-fashioned Won't-Pick-Up-Toys Cure and her Slow-Eater-Tiny-Bite-Taker Cure. (See others in the series.)

★*Mufaro's Beautiful Daughters* by John Steptoe. Lothrop 1987 (32p) In this African tale, Mufaro's daughters, kind Nyasha and spoiled Manyara, are invited to visit the king when he decides to take a wife.

My Grandmother's Stories: A Collection of Jewish Folk Tales by Adèle Geras. Knopf 1990 (96p) Everyday situations remind Grandmother of the ten folktales she retells in this collection.

Paddle to the Sea by Holling Clancy Holling. Houghton 1941 (64p) A young Canadian boy carves a canoe he calls Paddle-to-the-Sea and sets off through the Great Lakes to the sea.

★**Pass It On: African American Poetry for Children** by Wade Hudson. Scholastic 1993 (32p) This poetry collection presents fourteen African American poets, including Langston Hughes and Eloise Greenfield.

Pigs Aplenty, Pigs Galore by David McPhail. Dutton 1993 (32p) As the narrator tries to read, several pigs wreak havoc in his home.

The **Ramona** books by Beverly Cleary. Morrow The popular series about Ramona Quimby begins with four-year-old Ramona in **Beezus and Ramona.** (See others in the series.) *Many of the* Ramona *books are available in Spanish.*

Taxicab Tales by Barbara Ann Porte. Greenwillow 1992 (56p) Abigail and Sam's father always has wonderful tales to tell about his day as a taxicab driver.

The True Story of the Three Little Pigs by Jon Scieszka. Viking 1991 (32p) A. Wolf tells *his* side of the story, indicating that he was framed, in this highly original takeoff of the traditional tale. *Available in Spanish as* Verdadera historia de los tres cerditos.

The Trumpet of the Swan by E. B. White. Harper 1970 (210p) Louis the trumpeter swan lacks a voice, so he learns to play the trumpet to woo the beautiful Serena. *Available in Spanish as* La trompeta del cisne.

The Wind in the Willows by Kenneth Grahame. Scribners 1908 (254p) The story of Toad, Rat, Mole, and Badger has become one of the best-loved children's stories of all time. *Available in Spanish as* El viento en los sauces.

★**Yeh-shen: A Chinese Cinderella Story From China** by Ai Ling Louie. Philomel 1982 (32p) A young Chinese girl marries the prince despite objections and trickery by her stepmother and stepsisters.

Here are two excellent resources for selecting books.

The Read-Aloud Handbook, Fourth Edition by Jim Trelease. Viking Penguin 1995 (320p) This is the latest edition of the now-classic readaloud treasury.

The Parent's Guide to Storytelling by Margaret Read MacDonald. HarperCollins 1995 (128p) Subtitled "How to Make Up New Stories and Retell Old Ones," this guide includes hints and techniques in storytelling. Included also are bedtime stories, folktales, and storytime activities.

Sharing Family Stories

What are Family Stories?

Family stories are narratives in which the child and/or other family members are the featured characters. Every family has its own stories to tell. Their stories may be about everyday experiences, about special events, or about the family's history.

What is the Value of Sharing Family Stories?

When children work with their families to tell their stories, children, parents, and teachers all benefit.

- Sharing stories helps to create a bond between the child and his or her family.
- Children are motivated and perform better because these activities are meaningful to them.
- As teachers hear the stories of their students' families, they come to know the students and their families better.

Getting Started

There are a number of ways to include family stories in your curriculum. You may choose to implement a very elaborate program in which times are scheduled for you to work with families, first helping them to select topics to write about, and then helping them to draft, write, revise, and publish their stories. Some of the reference materials listed at the end of this article can be used to help you create such a program. Or, you may prefer simply to suggest ideas that will engage families in working together to tell or write their stories. What follows are suggestions and ideas for involving children and families in sharing their stories.

Help Children Collect Stories to Tell

You might want to begin by scheduling storytelling periods in your classroom. Some children will already have a wealth of family stories to share, but provide time for all students to gather information for their stories. Remind students that their parents, grandparents, aunts, and uncles can all be sources of stories.

Work with children to develop a list of topics about themselves and their families that they would like a family member to tell them about. If needed, suggest the following prompts:

- Tell me about something funny that I did when I was little.
- Tell me about something naughty that I did when I was little.
- Tell me about the funniest thing that has ever happened to our family.
- What was the scariest thing?
- Have we always lived in this neighborhood? Where else have we lived? Tell me about it.
- How did you learn to read?
- What did you like best about school?
- What was your favorite thing to do when you were little?
- Tell me about the place where you grew up. Who were your neighbors? What kinds of things did you do in your neighborhood?
- Tell me about a time you got into trouble.

Another way that children can learn stories about their families is to look through family photographs with a family member. Suggest that children find photographs of weddings, birthdays, vacations, or holiday celebrations that seem interesting, and ask the family member to tell them about the event.

After the adult has recounted the family story, suggest that the child practice retelling the story to the original storyteller. This will help the child clarify information and make him or her feel comfortable sharing the story with classmates.

Invite Families to Tell Stories

Throughout the year, issue a variety of open invitations for families to come to school to share their stories with the class. Parents who are not fluent in English may prefer to tell their stories through a translator. If obligations prevent interested family members from coming to school, you might want to arrange for them to audiotape or videotape their stories. It is important that you be accepting of any level of participation. Once one family decides to participate in a project and share a story with the class, other children will become very excited, and it will be easier to involve other parents.

Create a Book of Family Stories

You may find that children are interested in preserving some of their family stories in writing. One way they can do this is to ask their parents to help them write a family story for a class book. You might ask all families to write on the same topic, or you may prefer to have them select their own topic. Here are some suggestions for topics that families might write about:

- Their family history
- Favorite family customs and traditions
- Funny, scary, or unusual family times
- Family sayings and how they got started
- Family reunions

Children's literature can serve as a springboard or model for families' written stories. Reading stories about other families will help students and their families see how normal daily activities become the focus for interesting and memorable family stories. There are a number of wonderful stories written about families. Here are the titles of some that can be found in the students' anthology.

Enjoy

- *Family Pictures/Cuadros de familia* by Carmen Lomas Garza

Celebrate

- *Ramona and Her Mother* by Beverly Cleary

Encourage parents and/or children to illustrate their entries with pictures, photographs, or mementos that help tell their story.

Compile all of the family stories into a book. You might want to arrange a celebration where family members come to school to listen to the stories being read. After the stories have been shared, place the book in the class library, and allow students to read it as often as they like. If possible, make a copy of the book to send home for families to enjoy.

Using Graphics to Tell a Story

Sometimes the best way to tell a story is through art or graphics. For example, a class can create a large map of the world and invite families to mark on the map where they live now, and where they or past generations have lived before. Photographs or post cards of these places could be posted on the map. The child and his or her family might want to write a story that tells about the place.

Another idea is to create a class family quilt on cloth or on paper. Assign each family a "square" in which to "tell a story" in any way they like. You might suggest that they include drawings, photographs, or other mementos in their square. Each child and his or her family might then write a story that tells about their square. The information could be compiled into a book titled *Our Family Quilt*.

The key to successful sharing of family stories to is offer a variety of ways for families and children to work together to tell their stories. The results will be well worth the effort.

Related Readings

Building Communities of Learners: A Collaboration among Teachers, Students, Families, and Community, Sudia Paloma McCaleb. St. Martin's Press, New York, 1994. Family stories validate children's home cultures, showing families as protagonists who express the value of their own voice, opinion, and knowledge.

"Family Stories," Rita Buchoff. *The Reading Teacher,* Vol. 49, No. 3, November 1995, p. 230. Family stories help students to learn more about their heritage, to acquire literacy skills, and to respect the multicultural differences that make everyone unique.

"Listening to Family Stories Helps Teachers to Forge Ties," Jean Caldwell. *The Boston Sunday Globe,* July 30, 1995, p.88. In a program in Springfield, Massachusetts, teachers worked with families to tell their stories.

Conducting a Workshop

To build relationships with parents and to provide training for the group of volunteers willing to work with your class, you might want to conduct a workshop. For example, you might want to offer a workshop to launch the Family Reading Program or to train classroom volunteers. Workshops might focus on such topics as assisting with homework, helping the struggling reader, encouraging students to write, and developing positive parenting practices. Whatever your topic, the suggestions below should help to ensure your workshop's success.

Choosing a Time and Place

Scheduling a workshop in conjunction with a Back-to-School Night or Open House can increase attendance, as many parents usually attend these events. Holding the workshop early in the year gives everyone a chance to get the most out of the training. Some workshops, however, will need to occur later in the year, after you have had a chance to develop specific projects and to approach people about participating. Once you decide when to hold your workshop, you can increase attendance by:

- choosing a time slot that allows people to have dinner before arriving, and still get home from the workshop at a reasonable time.

- providing potential participants with an agenda so that they can see the amount of time involved and how the time will be spent. (30 to 45 minutes should be a sufficient amount of time for most workshops.)

- offering supervised child care for young children who accompany their parents.

Choose a site for your workshop that will create the right atmosphere. Media Centers and libraries are popular choices. Keep in mind, however, that students' desks and chairs don't make the most comfortable seating for adults. If other seating can be arranged, it will benefit participants' attitude and ability to focus. If you are offering child care, it is best to arrange for a separate room, so that your participants will not be distracted.

Inviting Participants

Here are some suggestions for your invitations:

- Use brightly colored paper to grab attention and keep the invitation from getting misplaced among other papers.

- Make the tone warm and informal to ease the anxieties of parents who may not have had positive experiences with school visits in the past.

- Mention any incentives that will increase attendance, such as refreshments, door prizes, and child care.

- Address them to parents, organizations, or other potential participants by name whenever possible.

- If possible, offer interpreters for parents who do not speak English, or encourage parents to bring their own interpreters.

- Request a response by a specific date, or explain that you'll be making follow-up phone calls, so that you'll know how many people to expect.

Gathering Materials

The topic for your workshop will determine the specific materials you'll need. Here is a list of materials to have on hand for all workshops:

- name tags and broad-tipped markers

- notepads and pens for participants to take notes

- toys, coloring books, crayons, etc., for child care if you're providing it

- refreshments

Planning the Agenda

Here is a sample agenda that can be used to plan any workshop:

Part I: Welcome (10 minutes)

Open the workshop with greetings and introductions. Provide a brief review of the agenda so that participants will know what to expect. Begin with a mixer that will help participants meet and talk to those seated around them, even if it is just to introduce themselves and tell their children's names and grade levels.

Part II: Explanation/demonstration of program or topic (20 minutes)

This part of the workshop will be most successful if participants are actively involved in doing or making something. The time segments listed are just suggestions and are not meant to limit you if you find the segments should be shorter or longer.

Break   (5–10 minutes)

Invite participants to get up and move about. Direct them to the refreshment table, and let them know the location of open bathrooms.

Part III: Discussion (10 minutes)

Encourage participants to ask questions and raise concerns. End on a positive note. Tell them what the next steps are or what will happen as a result of their participation.

Following Up

After the workshop, and once participants have undertaken a program, they may have valuable observations to share. Arrange for a way to exchange updates and feedback. You might discuss the program during parent-teacher conferences, or suggest using the Parent-Teacher-Child Dialogue form on pages 73 and 74. You may also wish to encourage participants to call you if questions or concerns arise.

Related Reading

Leamos! Let's Read! Parent-Meeting Leader's Guide, Mary and Richard Behn. ERIC Clearinghouse on Reading, English, and Communications, 1994. This English/Spanish guide provides the materials a teacher needs to conduct a workshop on how parents can help their children become better learners.

The Parent Project: A Workshop Approach to Parent Involvement, by James Vopat. Stenhouse Publishers, 1994. This accessible guide explains how to conduct a variety of workshops that foster parent involvement and parent/child/teacher communication.

Setting Up a Parent Resource Center

A Parent Resource Center is a special place in the school where parents can wait for their children, pick up something to read, or check out materials geared toward helping their children with school.

Many parents would welcome help in providing home support for their children's studies. For example, some parents may want more information to help them better understand their children's individual learning development and needs. Other parents would appreciate access to materials that help them enrich their children's home life, such as art materials or calculators. Still others may want background information on the topics their children are studying in order to engage them in conversation and exploration. A Parent Resource Center can help address these needs.

Meeting Parents' Needs

A typical Parent Resource Center can provide the following in-depth information on child development and special needs:

- pamphlets from organizations that specialize in children with special needs
- listings of community resources
- copies of the school's mission statement and district curriculum frameworks
- books, magazines, and clippings on general parenting information, child development, learning styles, special abilities, and challenges some learners face
- videotapes on educational topics

It can provide materials such as the following that may not be readily available in all homes:

- math manipulatives
- calculators and computers
- science equipment such as magnifying glasses, magnets, thermometers, and rain gauges
- rhythm instruments
- art supplies
- puzzles and games

A Parent Resource Center can also provide special materials that tie into themes in individual classes:

- fiction and nonfiction books for adults
- extra copies of curriculum materials used in the classroom
- other theme-related materials and activity lists

Some Parent Resource Centers conduct classes or workshops for parents and refer parents to social services and child care.

Getting Ready to Open

Be sure to involve parents and staff in planning and setting up the Parent Resource Center. Besides determining the mission of your center, you'll need to address where the center will be, when it will be open, who will staff it, and how you will obtain materials for it. Here is a suggested "action plan":

- Decide first on the mission of the center and put it in writing. This information can then be included when you are ready to advertise the center's availability.

- Decide where you will house your center. This might be a small unused classroom, a section of the library or media center, or a space near the main entrance or school office. Comfortable chairs, house plants, and a coffee pot will help parents feel especially welcome.

- Decide who will be responsible for greeting and assisting parents, keeping materials in order, and tracking any materials signed out. The parent-teacher association may be able to provide volunteers or funding for a part-time staff.

- Decide what materials you will have and which, if any, can be signed out. Consult your school librarian or Parent Resource Center personnel about an efficient sign-out system for materials that will be available for lending.

Obtaining Materials

To obtain the materials and resources you need, make a "wish list" and publicize your needs. Take advantage of:

- **Donations.** Contact parents, office and art supply stores, and local bookstores. The education departments at local colleges or universities may also be willing to donate or lend materials.

- **Fund-raising.** Some schools have raised money through the parent-teacher association or through student-involved efforts such as magazine drives.

- **Free materials from professional organizations.** Here are some sources:

   American Library Association
   50 East Huron Street
   Chicago, IL 60611

   International Reading Association
   P.O. Box 8130
   Newark, DE 19714

   National Council for Teachers of English
   Order Department
   111 Kenyon Road
   Urbana, IL 61801

   Reading Is Fundamental, Inc.
   Publications Department
   600 Maryland Avenue, S.W.
   Washington, DC 20024

Advertising Your Center

It is important to remind parents on an ongoing basis of the availability of the center and new items in it. Let parents know about the materials in the center and the hours it is open. When advertising, you might also want to include updated "wish lists" to replenish consumable supplies. Here are some things you might try:

- Send home a letter or brochure detailing the materials available and inviting parents to drop by. If possible, list times when parents can meet informally with the principal in the center.

- Run notices in the school newsletter, highlighting different materials each time.

- Post flyers on bulletin boards near the main entrance and in the school office.

- Contact local banks, places of worship, community centers, hospitals, libraries, and radio and cable television stations. They will often provide free public service announcements including messages on electronic bulletin boards.

Working with the Community

What the Community Can Provide

A major computer company donates computers to schools in the state where it has a large plant. A group of local businesspeople volunteer to come into the classroom and talk about their jobs. An ice-cream company provides ice cream to local schools for fundraising. An insurance company donates binders so that students can collect their writing for the statewide portfolio assessment. Businesspeople serve on the state board of education. Across the country, people are actively working to forge links between business and education.

Every city or town in our nation has resources to draw upon to make school-community links. The general kinds of support that community members can provide in almost any community include financial resources, materials, and volunteer services.

Financial Resources Sometimes businesses are willing to make direct donations to schools, especially if there is a well-defined purpose and rationale for using the funds. The most successful links have a clear tie between the business and an educational purpose. Let's say, for example, you're trying to raise enough money to start a student magazine. If your school or district policies allow, you might solicit funds from magazine publishers or printers in your state.

The finished product would carry a line of thanks recognizing the source of the donation.

Donated Materials When you identify a particular need, try to locate a local business that might benefit in some way from fulfilling your need. For example, in one community, a local bookstore donates books at cost for the school book fair. The school's Parent-Teacher Association gets the profit from the sales. In return, the bookstore, which also supplies store bags, receives favorable publicity among prospective customers. In many cases, businesses can write off the cost of the donated items. In any case, the publicity serves to enhance the company's reputation and can pay off in future sales.

Volunteers In some communities, local businesses adopt a particular grade level or class. Employees can serve that class as tutors or mentors—whatever suits the needs of the students and the talents of the employees. Other good candidates for volunteers include high school students, who can sometimes get credit for tutoring, and college students hoping to broaden their teaching background. Retired teachers and other senior citizens may enjoy passing on knowledge and skills to young people. Any volunteer who works directly with students should always be supervised by a licensed educator.

Field Trip Destination Get permission to visit businesses to foster students' awareness of literacy in action. Students may be surprised to find how important reading and writing are as they observe salespeople consulting brochures and filling out forms, travel agents consulting computers, lawyers researching cases, or auto mechanics consulting repair manuals.

Speakers Anyone who can demonstrate the importance of literacy on the job is a valuable speaker. Begin by asking parents of students in your class if they or their coworkers could speak to the class. Other possibilities include a local news anchor, sportswriter, meteorologist, town clerk, city manager, or hospital worker. Organizations such as the Rotary Club may have a list of members who regularly speak about their careers to schoolchildren. Before the visit, make sure the speaker can relate to students at a grade-appropriate level. Afterward, help students send personal letters of thanks to the speaker.

Showcase Another role a business can take is to set aside a hall or bulletin board on its premises as a showcase for student work. Students' written reflections and artwork based on employees' visits to their classroom can provide positive feedback for speakers, tutors, and mentors. Many public locations, such as banks, airports, and hospitals, offer a chance for community members to view and appreciate student writing.

How to Approach Community Members

Businesses Network with parents and use personal contacts whenever you can. If you don't have a ready connection with a particular business or group you've targeted, a business letter, carefully written and edited by the class, or a phone call is the best bet for contacting them.

When approaching businesses, make sure you are contacting the proper department and person. Explain clearly why you have contacted them and what return they will receive for their investment. Be precise in your request, and be prepared to turn to another resource if they are unable to help.

College Students Contact the person in charge of teacher training or the student teacher supervisor. Find out what the curriculum and field-based needs are for specific classes. Be specific about your needs—how many volunteers, how often, how many hours, and for what tasks.

High School Students High school guidance counselors and English teachers can let you know of good candidates for tutors. To make their transportation arrangements easier, you may wish to schedule several tutors from the same school for the same time.

Retired Teachers/Senior Citizens Contact this rich resource through associations such as your local Council on Aging. You can also take out an ad in the newspaper, run a radio ad, or put in a plea on the local cable television access channel. It is a good idea to find out potential volunteers' expertise and use their services in the areas in which they are most comfortable.

Public Acknowledgment Whatever the source of school-community partnerships, public thanks are essential. There are many ways to express your appreciation. Consider end-of-year celebrations for volunteers. Write thank-you letters to follow up on field trips. Send letters to the editor of your local newspaper about the contributions of individuals and organizations. Ask the local newspaper and cable television station to send in a reporter and a photographer to cover special events. Keep parents informed through the school newsletter. Making your thanks public will keep the partnerships growing.

Related Reading

"Book Buddies: Creating enthusiasm for literacy learning," Karen Bromley, Deborah Winters, and Kerri Schlimmer. *The Reading Teacher*, Vol. 47, No. 5, February 1994, p. 392. University students of education and at-risk youngsters collaborate on reading folktales and writing journals.

"Working with parents: Beyond parents and into the community," Timothy V. Rasinski and Anthony D. Fredericks. *The Reading Teacher*, Vol. 44, No. 9, May 1991, p. 698. Respected educators describe specific ways to integrate classrooms with the community.

Starting a Homework Club

A Homework Club provides students with a place to do homework where an adult will monitor and guide their efforts. Homework Clubs often meet one or two days a week. They are usually supervised by teachers or volunteers. Once the Homework Club is established, keep asking for parents' and students' ideas on how it can better serve their needs.

Getting Started

You might want to meet with parents and students first to determine the purpose or scope of your Homework Club, as well as to plan the location, schedule, staffing, and resources. This meeting may also help you identify parents who may be willing to help.

Scope

What you can offer will be determined by available staff, students' needs, and the resources you can obtain. In some clubs, teachers offer coaching and instructional support for students. If you have access to reference books and computers, students will also be able to do research and word-processing tasks.

Some Homework Clubs provide incentives to students who maintain or improve their school performance, or who attend regularly. You might want to set up a system whereby students earn an appropriate reward.

Location

A school location is most practical for everyone. The number and ages of students involved, as well as availability of your staff, will determine the number of rooms needed. The most basic requirement is that the location(s) have sufficient chairs and tables or desks.

Schedule

Before deciding on a schedule, consider any competing activities, as well as transportation problems. Also consider whether an early morning program would better serve students and parents. You might start by offering your Homework Club one day a week, then expand it. Since schedules for club members may deviate from the normal school schedule, you may need to obtain parental permission for these students. You may also need to obtain permission to sign out students whose transportation arrangements are different on other school days.

Staffing

It is desirable to engage the support of a number of teachers so that the responsibility can be shared. In addition to teachers or other trained staff, consider adding volunteers. Encourage parents, grandparents and local retired people, high school and college students to participate. Peer tutors can also provide useful assistance. You might provide workshops to train volunteers. Keep in mind that volunteers should be supervised by trained staff.

Resources

This is a good opportunity to involve parents and the community. Put out the word that you are seeking donations of books, materials, and equipment. A parent may work for a business that would be willing to donate a used computer. Businesses are also good sources of large amounts of usable scrap paper. Ask the librarians at your public library when they replace encyclopedia sets and other reference books to see if you can "take them off their hands." A local doctor's office may be happy to turn over old issues of news and children's magazines. And everyone can be on the alert for books at garage or library sales, or at home.

Assessing Your Home/Community Program

This form is to help you assess your home/community program. Your answers to the questions below, for each section or parts of a section of *Home/Community Connections* that you used, should prove helpful in assessing your home/community program this year—and in setting your goals for the coming year.

Section 1: Communicating with Parents

1. How would you assess your attempts to communicate with parents?
   - ❏ Very Successful
   - ❏ Somewhat Successful
   - ❏ Unsuccessful

2. How do you think your communications with parents affected your students' achievement?
   - ❏ Had a Positive Effect
   - ❏ Had No Effect
   - ❏ Unsure of the Effect

3. How could your communications with parents be improved?

   _____

   _____

Section 2: Parents and Teachers Working as Partners

1. How would you assess your attempts to involve parents actively in their child's education?
   - ❏ Very Successful
   - ❏ Somewhat Successful
   - ❏ Unsuccessful

2. How did your attempts at actively involving parents affect your students' achievement?
   - ❏ Had a Positive Effect
   - ❏ Had No Effect
   - ❏ Unsure of the Effect

3. How could you improve parents' involvement in their child's education?

   _____

   _____

Section 3: Using Volunteers in the Classroom

1. How would you assess your attempts at involving volunteers in the classroom?
   - ❏ Very Successful
   - ❏ Somewhat Successful
   - ❏ Unsuccessful

2. How did your classroom volunteer program affect your students' achievement?
   - ❏ Had a Positive Effect
   - ❏ Had No Effect
   - ❏ Unsure of the Effect

3. How easy or difficult was it for you to manage volunteers in the classroom?
   - ❏ Very Easy
   - ❏ Easy
   - ❏ Difficult
   - ❏ Very Difficult

4. How could you improve your classroom volunteer program?

   _____

   _____

Section 4: Moving Beyond the Classroom

1. Which, if any, of the following programs did you implement?
   - ❏ Family Reading Program
   - ❏ Parent Resource Center
   - ❏ Homework Club
   - ❏ Working with the Community

2. How successful were you in getting parents, children, and/or community members to commit to the program(s)?
   - ❏ Very Successful
   - ❏ Somewhat Successful
   - ❏ Unsuccessful

3. How do you think the program(s) affected students' reading achievement?
   - ❏ Had a Positive Effect
   - ❏ Had No Effect
   - ❏ Unsure of the Effect

4. If you were to implement the program(s) again, how could you improve it/them?

   _____

   _____

   _____

   _____